Advance Praise for

The Totally Sweet '90s

"Mr. Dewey gives *The Totally Sweet '90s* an A+! Should be on the required reading list for all Baysiders. But don't worry, no need for caffeine pills, Jesse. Each page is a delightful reminiscence of that sometimes glorious but all too often ignominious (look it up, slacker) decade that polished off the twentieth century."

—Patrick O'Brien, actor from *Saved by the Bell*

THE
TOTALLY
SWEET '90s

*From Clear Cola to Furby, and Grunge
to "Whatever," the Toys, Tastes, and Trends
That Defined a Decade*

**Gael Fashingbauer Cooper
and Brian Bellmont**

A PERIGEE BOOK

A PERIGEE BOOK
Published by the Penguin Group
Penguin Group (USA) Inc.
375 Hudson Street, New York, New York 10014, USA

USA | Canada | UK | Ireland | Australia | New Zealand | India | South Africa | China

Penguin Books Ltd., Registered Offices: 80 Strand, London WC2R 0RL, England
For more information about the Penguin Group, visit penguin.com.

Library of Congress Cataloging-in-Publication Data

Cooper, Gael Fashingbauer.
The totally sweet '90s : from clear cola to Furby, and grunge to "whatever," the toys, tastes, and trends
that defined a decade / Gael Fashingbauer Cooper and Brian Bellmont.
pages cm
"A Perigee Book."
Includes index.
ISBN 978-0-399-16004-2
1. Popular culture—United States—History—20th century.   2. United States—Social life and
customs—1971–   3. Nineteen nineties.   I. Bellmont, Brian.   II. Title.
E169.Z82C675   2013
973.929—dc23   2013000219

First edition: June 2013

PRINTED IN THE UNITED STATES OF AMERICA

10   9   8   7   6   5   4   3   2   1

Text design by Tiffany Estreicher

Most Perigee books are available at special quantity discounts for bulk purchases
for sales promotions, premiums, fund-raising, or educational use. Special books,
or book excerpts, can also be created to fit specific needs. For details, write:
Special.Markets@us.penguingroup.com.

This one's for our siblings—
Rudge, Claudia, Drew, Clio, Anne,
and Dave on Gael's side,
and Mike, Dave, and Kevin on Brian's.

And also for the friends who helped us survive and thrive in the 1990s.
For Gael, that's Lisa Olchefske Gilbert, Sue Dillon, Bob Seabold and
Bobbe Norenberg, Scott and Stacy Pampuch, Todd Mannis, Dan Dosen,
Scott Feraro, and Matt Gillen. For Brian, that would be Chris Moore,
Mike Zipko, Kathleen Hennessy, Dave Aeikens, and all the folks
at WEAU, CONUS, Axiom, and Shandwick.

Kids of the '90s, Unite!

We know, you've spent a lifetime celebrating the nostalgia of older generations. Every other week a magazine cover remembers the enormous social changes of the 1960s, a shaggy 1970s band goes on tour, or a hideous fashion trend of the 1980s returns. That's all well and good, even if jelly shoes haven't gotten any more comfortable in thirty years.

But maybe you still smile when you hear someone mention *The Oregon Trail*, or when you find your old Lisa Frank notebook in your mom's closet. Or maybe you get sucked in to watching the entire *Big Lebowski* every time it pops up on cable. Or you can't bear to throw away your cassette tapes, even though you haven't owned a tape player for years. There's nothing wrong with holding fond memories of your own chosen decade—even if you still can't figure out why Urkel was ever popular.

The reason we wrote this book—and its 1970s–1980s-themed predecessor, *Whatever Happened to Pudding Pops?*—is that we believe the lost toys, tastes, and trends of an era do more than just remind us of what we liked as kids. They tell us a lot about who we were then, and who we are today. You can't figure out where you're going until you understand how you got there.

Sure, each decade is technically just ten years, but we feel confident saying that the twentieth century seemed to gain speed as it neared its end. Starting in the 1990s, technology jumped on a roller-coaster-fast track that changed everything. Mobile phones went from brick-sized behemoths that only Gordon Gekko carried to slim little numbers that everyone from nannies to nuns popped in their pockets. Televisions used to be so clunky they might have singlehandedly made you refuse to help a friend move. After the '90s technology revolution, they morphed into sexy flat screens that hung on walls like paintings.

Before the 1990s began, you may not have received a single email. By 2000, the dude who lived in your AOL inbox was barking "You've got mail!" every couple of minutes.

It's not just that the 1990s introduced us to a boatload of new stuff—all decades do that. It's the fact that items we first encountered in the '90s didn't just come and go. Computers, mobile phones, electronic news and communications—these things may keep changing form, but they're never going to fade out of our lives completely, not now. They'll get better—or weirder—but for good or for ill, they're here to stay.

Also in the '90s, many of the things generations had grown up with started to slip away. Photographic film. Landlines. Newspapers. You almost don't notice when those things start to slowly roll out of your life, but when you look back at where you were in 1990 versus where you were in 1999, it's mind-blowing.

Technology aside, it was a decade of rich creativity and downright crazy inventions. Just think about how the 1990s loved to play with form.

You think you had candy, previous generations? We have super-sour candy that will rip a layer off your tongue! Think T-shirts pretty much can't be improved? We have shirts that change color with the temperature! Thirsty? We have clear colas and beverages with weird floating pearls in them! You've seen dozens of movies and watched a million hours of TV? We're going to hit you with Quentin Tarantino's pop-culture-flavored violence and the whole bizarre reality TV universe. What's that Al Jolson said as Hollywood moved into talkies? You ain't heard nothin' yet, indeed.

As advanced and futuristic as we thought we were back in the 1990s, we look back on it now as a decade of innocence. The Berlin Wall came down, the Soviet Union imploded, and for a brief moment the nuclear fears that haunted '80s kids almost fell away. We had no idea, as we sailed into airports an hour before a flight, cruising through metal detectors with shoes and belts on, tweezers and giant bottles of mouthwash stowed in our carry-ons, what the 2000s would bring.

What happened to the gentle memories of our youth? Some vanished totally, like the craze for clear colas. Some stayed around, but faded from the spotlight, like *America's Funniest Home Videos* and the bungee-jumping fad. Some temporarily disappeared, were revised, and reintroduced . . . but you'll have to read the book to find out which ones. Not everything we remember here was invented in the 1990s, but it was important to us then. And since you're flipping through this book, we're guessing it was important to you too.

So don't let anyone tell you it's too early to remember the 1990s. Smear on some body glitter and put some fresh batteries in your Big Mouth Billy Bass. We're heading back to the era when clear cola seemed somehow cool, we all knew how to fix a cassette tape with a pencil, and TGIF and SNICK ruled the airwaves.

Grab some Dunkaroos and pump it up, Kris. This is your so-called life.

Adam Sandler Songs on *Saturday Night Live*

Ambitious cast members on *Saturday Night Live* always find new ways to stand out. In the 1990s, Mike Myers had *Wayne's World*, Chris Farley played lovable chubby losers, and Adam Sandler, long before he was a movie star, hit the right note with his own original songs.

Sandler's topics were truly off the wall. His "Thanksgiving Song" mixed completely random pop-culture lines with tales from Turkey Day itself ("Turkey for you and turkey for me/Can't believe Tyson gave that girl VD"), while his "Hanukkah Song" listed famous Jews who celebrate the holiday. ("Guess who eats together at the Carnegie Deli? Bowser from Sha Na Na and Arthur Fonzarelli!") And he wasn't afraid to rhyme "Hanukkah" with "marijuanica."

Perhaps Sandler's best-loved *SNL* song is the one Farley helped him perform, "Lunch Lady Land." Farley was perfect as the mole-sporting, hair-netted worker who's the Simon Legree of cafeteria food—until the pizza and pudding came out for revenge. On a show where sketches often run groaningly long, seeing Sandler bring out his guitar meant a guaranteed two minutes of the purest and most joyful laughter.

STATUS: Sandler's moved on to movies. His role as the *SNL* songwriter was eventually filled by Andy Samberg and his Lonely Island crew, singing about cupcakes and the Chronicles of Narnia and gift-wrapping one's genitals.

The Adventures of Pete & Pete

Before *Yo Gabba Gabba!*, the show every indie hipster wanted to guest star on was *The Adventures of Pete & Pete*. And no wonder—if you were Iggy Pop, Debbie Harry, or Michael Stipe, wouldn't you kill to be on the coolest, weirdest, most surreal program of the '90s? Ostensibly about two carrot-topped brothers, Big Pete and Little Pete ("Get a life, jerkweed!" was one of the littler Pete's favorite put-downs) the Nickelodeon show was like nothing else on TV—and certainly like nothing else on Nickelodeon, which had traditionally run more, uh, lowbrow fare. (Cough—*Hey Dude*.)

The Adventures of Pete & Pete was an oddball offering about school, suburbia, and subversion. Little Pete was an anti-authority nut with a tattoo of an adult woman (Petunia!) on his forearm. The boys' mom had a metal plate in her head. They hung out with the neighborhood superhero, Artie, who described himself as "the strongest man . . . in the world!" Luscious Jackson played at their prom. And it kept getting weirder. And better than 99 percent of anything else on TV. In the immortal words of Little Pete, "Read it and weep, fungus-lick!"

STATUS: *Pete & Pete* started as minute-long short segments, then graduated to regular-show status from 1993–1996. The cast and crew reunited for an event in 2012.

FUN FACT: Toby Huss, who played Artie, went on to voice Cotton Hill and Kahn Souphanousinphone on *King of the Hill*.

America's Funniest Home Videos

Before YouTube, the only place you could check out embarrassing real-life video footage was on *America's Funniest Home Videos*, which kicked off in 1989 and quickly became *the* watercooler show of the '90s. "Oh, man—did you see that one of the kid smashing his dad in the nertz with a golf club? Classic. I wish I could post that on the Internet." "What's the Internet?" "No idea, but someone should totally invent it so we can watch that video over and over again."

Pretty soon, everybody with a camcorder—at that time, the giant kind you had to balance on your shoulder—was aiming it at any remotely dangerous or adorable situation, hoping to capture a pyramid of people collapsing into an alligator pit or a baby juggling Tasers.

Host Bob Saget and, later, folks like Daisy Fuentes and Tom Bergeron, delivered terrible patter in between clips, all set to an uncontrollable laugh track. Why? To make the often lame, overlit, grainy, and blurry videos more appealing? Good Lord, get to the deck collapse already.

Much has been made of the show's penchant for featuring people getting smacked in the groin. So much, in fact, that we won't belabor the conversation other to say the reputation was absolutely, rightfully, and painfully deserved. If the nutcup fits . . .

STATUS: Still going strong.

FUN FACT: In one audience-participation segment, "Head, Gut, or Groin," host Bergeron had members of the studio audience guess where the person in the next video would get whacked.

American Gladiators

I f aliens on their way to invade Earth had caught a few minutes of *American Gladiators*, they would have turned their ships around and headed right back to their home planet. Because who wanted to mess with an army of muscle-bound mutants, especially if they were armed with giant Q-tips? That was apparently the reason we all tuned in to the syndicated 1989–1997 hit: to watch regular Joes get their spandex-covered butts handed to them by freaks of nature with names like Nitro, Laser, Turbo, and Zap.

Contestants bobbed and weaved while Gladiators shot at them with one-hundred-mile-per-hour tennis-ball cannons. Why, it was just like the Olympics! Only not at all. But the commentators (including, in the first season, Joe Theismann) took this goofy game just as seriously, trying to keep a straight face while they interviewed a contestant who just got pulled off a rock wall by a shaved and oiled bodybuilder. With the breathless commentary, squeaky-clean heroes, and mwah-ha-ha villains, *Gladiators* pulled out all the stops to artificially amp up the drama wherever it could. But we all really knew it wasn't much more than a cut-rate pro-wrestling match mixed with a cheesy obstacle course. And that's exactly why we never missed an episode.

STATUS: The show came back in 2008, this time hosted by Hulk Hogan.

FUN FACT: Many of the audience members "watching" the Gladiators were actually just faces painted onto the set's walls.

Andrew "Dice" Clay

Hickory dickory dock . . ." Trust us, you don't want to hear the rest. With jet-black sideburns slashed across his cheeks and a cigarette permanently dangling from his lips, shock comic Andrew "Dice" Clay shot to national attention in 1988 with his stand-up comedy versions of nursery rhymes so obscene, they'd make Mother Goose lose her tail feathers.

He'd punctuate every punch line with a delighted "Oh!" like even he couldn't believe he'd said it. The Brooklyn-born comedian quickly gained a rep as a rude, crude misogynist, sparking protests from every possible angle. MTV banned him and his leather jacket for life in 1989, when he let loose a few of his expletive-packed poems on the MTV Video Music Awards. And when he was scheduled to host *Saturday Night Live* the next year, cast member Nora Dunn and musical guest Sinead O'Connor sat out the show in protest. Note to Dice: When someone who rips up a picture of the pope on national TV calls you out for being too controversial, you might want to dial it back a tad.

STATUS: In 2011, "Dice" played a fictionalized version of himself on HBO's *Entourage*, which jump-started his career yet again. MTV officially unbanned him the same year. Oh!

FUN FACT: Clay played the bouncer at Molly Ringwald's nighttime hangout in the 1986 movie *Pretty in Pink*.

Arch Deluxe

Fast-fooderies, know your place! McDonald's really shouldn't think of itself as an adult eatery. After all, hoity-toity steakhouses don't try to build locations in food courts or give away toy Smurfs.

In 1996, McDonald's decided to market certain food items strictly to grown-ups. Headlining the new sandwich line was the Arch Deluxe—kind of like a quarter pounder, but featuring lettuce, tomato, a mustard-mayo sauce, round bacon, and a really bready potato-flour bun.

The chain reportedly spent $100 million on a campaign straight out of your mom's reverse-psychology book. Kids hate these burgers, grown-ups! Doesn't that make you want to order a couple dozen? When those ads didn't bring customers flocking in, the company switched to commercials showing Ronald McDonald engaging in adult activities. Get your mind out of the gutter—he was golfing and nightclubbing. The less said about the carrot-topped clown boogeying down at a nightspot, the better.

The Deluxe line was reportedly one of the biggest corporate flops of all time. Wash one down with a New Coke while surfing your WebTV and you may have the perfect trifecta of capitalistic failure.

STATUS: The Arch Deluxe is gone, but McDonald's didn't give up on premium sandwiches, eventually adding Angus third-pound burgers to the menu.

FUN FACT: You can spot a young Jessica Biel in an Arch Deluxe ad.

Austin Stories

Only twelve episodes of *Austin Stories* were ever shown, but viewers too lazy to turn off MTV after *The Real World* ended discovered the 1997–1998 show and made it a cult classic.

Texas comics Brad "Chip" Pope, Howard Kremer, and Laura House played three friends of various degrees of Slackertude. Nerdy Chip couldn't hold down a job and mooned over the girlfriend who dumped him. ("Shhh, Angie's sleeping!" he scolded pals. "With that guy!") Lanky Howard was always working a scam, from hawking candy he found in the trash to selling his girlfriend's blood to get his impounded car back. Alt-weekly journalist Laura was the most responsible of the three, but even she wasn't above calling the Czech Republic on the newspaper's dime.

The charm of the cast and the non-Hollywood style of the setting earned raves, but MTV made *Austin* pretty much impossible to find, throwing other shows in its time slot with no warning. Then they canceled it for good, leaving the talented leads to move on to Hollywood, and fans to forever wonder if snagging a theater-employee vest from the thrift store would really earn you free movies for life.

STATUS: *Austin* told its last story in 1998. It's not the same, but IFC's *Portlandia* has a similarly quirky cast and regional setting.

FUN FACT: While MTV foolishly never released the show itself, Kremer sells autographed DVDs of the entire series on eBay.

"Baby Got Back"

In case you haven't heard, Sir Mix-A-Lot likes big butts, and he cannot lie. That's what he claimed in his 1992 smash Grammy-winning (!) single "Baby Got Back," anyway. And we believe him. He was pretty clear.

We're not exactly sure where Mix got the title "Sir," but we're guessing he didn't get knighted by the queen for the classy line "My anaconda don't want none unless you've got buns, hon." Still, while Her Royal Highness probably wasn't a fan, plenty of people were. The song sold more than two million copies, many of them to suburban kids named Ashley or Trevor who somehow felt the lyrics spoke to their white-bread, Nickelodeon lives: "Tell 'em to shake it! Shake it! Shake that healthy butt!"

The tune sparked a butt-load of controversy. Some people took it to be a straight-up tribute to women with large backsides, others called it antifeminist and protested Mix-A-Lot's concerts. Whatever the rationale, the tune sparked a whole new generation of musicians to sing songs about derrieres. You other brothers can't deny: The folks behind "Thong Song," "Rump Shaker," "Honky Tonk Badonkadonk," and "Da Butt" should give Sir Mix-A-Lot a giant, butt-shaped medal.

STATUS: The tune simply won't go away. In 2012, a YouTube video of a Sir Ian McKellen impersonator reading the lyrics as if they were Shakespearean sonnets made the Internet rounds.

FUN FACT: In 2009, Burger King took flak for a commercial for a SpongeBob SquarePants kids' meal that changed the lyrics to "I like square butts."

Baby-Sitters Club Books

Did every girl who read the Baby-Sitters Club books try to organize her own version of the group? Did anyone succeed? Sadly, our friends were neither as industrious nor as kid-competent as Kristy, Claudia, Mary Anne, Stacey, and the rest of Ann M. Martin's characters. And what kind of neighborhood did they live in where parents burned up the phone lines during one half-hour period trying to book preteens to babysit? When we kids tried the same thing, the only time the phone rang was with a wrong number.

Moms preferred Baby-Sitters Club books to Sweet Valley High novels because the Baby-Sitters weren't boy-crazy. But that doesn't

mean the books didn't tackle issues. From diabetes to divorce to detesting gym, the sitters grappled with all kinds of kid angst. Yet at the core of the group was a deep love and loyalty that rang true. Middle school can be agony, and if you couldn't find a solid pack of pals in your school lunchroom, you could at least read about one.

And oh, the fashions. Quirky Claudia led the way, but all of the girls had wardrobes that seemed alternately drool-worthy and disastrous. Red sneakers covered with beads and glitter? Denim jumpsuits? Purple harem pants paired with a green leotard and red belt? Good thing it wasn't the Fashion Designers Club.

STATUS: A prequel and updated versions of some of the books were published in 2010.

FUN FACT: In the updated books, mention of a cassette player was changed to "headphones" and a perm became "an expensive hairstyle."

Barney & Friends

With his dopey voice and incessant "I Love You" song, Barney the declawed dinosaur appealed to toddlers and college-age potheads alike when he lumbered onto PBS in 1992. Because why *wouldn't* you tune into a show about a vicious killing machine running a day care?

The purple T. rex would have had his felt-covered behind handed to him by a real prehistoric predator (or a small mouse), but you've

got to wonder what kind of parent would drop their kids off at a clubhouse to spend the day with a dinosaur—even one that looked like a minor-league baseball team mascot. The "Friends" of the title, green Triceratops Baby Bop, yellow Protoceratops B.J., and orange Hadrosaur Riff, were no Monica and Chandler either.

But 1990s kids loved Barney with the same passion they reserve for other things adults abhor, like SpaghettiO's with those weird little hot dogs or that "99 Bottles of Beer on the Wall" song. Speaking of songs, let us speak of the song. Even those blessed humans who'd never seen a single episode of *Barney* knew the song. I love you, you love me, this tune will make you go out of your tree.

STATUS: Reruns are still going strong, on PBS and DVD, though new episodes aren't being made.

FUN FACT: In 2009, *TV Guide* named *Barney & Friends* one of the worst shows ever.

Baywatch

If you're going to go swimming in Los Angeles, find somewhere to take a dip other than the strip of beach patrolled by the beautiful lifeguards of *Baywatch*. Unless you enjoy your suntan lotion mixed with murder, diamond smuggling, tropical storms, illegal offshore casinos, and giant octopuses, that is. It's a wonder the lifeguards had any time at all to rescue drowning swimmers, since they seemed to spend most of their days (and nights) fighting crime and natural disasters—and dealing with more pedestrian issues like dog-sitting, custody battles, and root canals. Also, oiling up their pecs.

The over-the-top plots were beside the point. Most of the show was an excuse to linger on jiggly, slow-motion shots of red-swimsuited lifeguard babes running in the sand. And David Hasselhoff and his hairy, bare chest (he's big in Germany, you know). The show made gigantic stars of its cast, especially Pamela Anderson and her cleavage. And it made Hasselhoff a very rich man. When *Baywatch* was initially canceled after just one season on NBC, the star put up his own money to launch it in syndication. Smart move: At its peak, more than a billion people a week all over the world tuned in. Slow-motion boobies apparently translate in any language.

STATUS: *Baywatch* stayed afloat for nine seasons, then morphed into *Baywatch Hawaii* for two more. From 2000 to 2002, a *Baywatch* spoof sitcom called *Son of the Beach*—produced by Howard Stern—aired on FX.

FUN FACT: In the much, much worse spinoff *Baywatch Nights*, The Hoff dealt with paranormal phenomena like time travel, vampires, and fish-women.

Beanie Babies

Let's hope your parents invested in Apple or Microsoft in the 1990s instead of putting your whole college fund in Beanie Babies. Everyone knew one aunt or cousin with an extra bedroom stuffed with the soft little beanbag animals, convinced that one of them was rare enough to be her magical lottery ticket to Mansionville. But since thousands of people thought the same thing, there were innumerable clones of Cheezer the Mouse or Dinky the Dodo out there, and nobody got rich.

Most of us didn't collect with dollar signs in our eyes, though—we just bought the ones we liked best. Who didn't swoop up the calico cat because it looked just like your own Jessica Patterpaws, or take home Princess, the Princess Diana bear, because you were still mad about Prince Charles cheating on Di with Camilla?

The Ty toy company was brilliant when it came to reeling us in. Each animal not only had a name, but a birthday and, oddly enough, a poem. A poorly written poem, with uneven meter, that might rhyme "swim" with "fins," but a poem nonetheless.

If you were a collector, your fun was pretty much limited to dusting the things now and then and screeching at anyone who tried to remove the all-important hang tag. If you were just a kid, Beanies provided you with a fun, animal-centric world, where manatees hung out with huskies and unicorns shared room space with tyrannosaurs, like a weird and wonderful zoo with no bars. Or logic.

STATUS: The original Beanie Babies line was "retired" in 2008 but brought back a year later.

FUN FACT: In 2009, a Bo the Portuguese Water Dog Beanie Baby was issued to honor President Barack Obama's pet.

Beavis and Butt-Head

It's every bad American teen stereotype put into an amplifier and cranked up to eleven. In the spaces where Beavis and Butt-Head's brains should be, you'll find convenience-store burritos, a love of fire and bad heavy metal, and a million variations on the word "buttmunch."

But for being such dumb kids, B&B smartly channeled their inner *Mystery Science Theater 3000* when it came to dissing music videos. Watching Kiss, Butt-Head declares: "These guys are pretty cool for a bunch of mimes." Perplexed during Nirvana's "Smells Like Teen Spirit," he asks Beavis: "Is this, like, grudge music?" And say what you will about their opinions, their music criticism was often spot-on. In one segment, they watch Milli Vanilli for several seconds in complete horror, before changing the channel to Journey without saying a word.

STATUS: The show originally ran from 1993–1997, then was revived in 2011. In addition to videos, they now mock episodes of *Jersey Shore* and even UFC fights.

FUN FACT: On the show, Beavis's shirt says "Metallica" and Butt-Head's says "AC/DC," but in other merchandise, for trademark reasons, the shirts read, respectively, "Death Rock" and "Skull."

Bee Girl

Maybe the Bee Girl of Blind Melon's 1991 "No Rain" video was an early metaphor for how the decade would progress. You remember: Gawky ten-year-old Heather DeLoach is laughed at for her dowdy appearance and clunky tap dance. Bravely, she keeps on trying, and eventually joyously stumbles upon a sunny green field full of outsider bees just like her.

So too the 1980s, full of slick Madonna and Duran Duran videos, poofy shoulder pads and elaborate hair, were giving way to the sloppier, more laid-back flannels and garage-band aesthetic of grunge and riot grrrls. Suddenly the cheerleaders and jocks no longer ruled, the burnouts and nerds were ascendant. For a while at least, it seemed as if the entertainment world was realizing that there were more imperfect originals than cookie-cutter pop princesses.

Things didn't end happily for Blind Melon lead singer Shannon Hoon, though, who according to VH1's *Behind the Music* was high on acid during the "No Rain" video. He died of a cocaine overdose in 1995, leaving a baby daughter who'd never know him and a band that would only have that one big hit. The '90s might indeed have been a more accepting decade for misfits, but that doesn't mean they lacked for casualties.

STATUS: As MTV transformed from a music station to a reality TV network, catchy music videos were all but replaced by catchy Internet viral videos. Cute cats and kids who've just been to the dentist, anyone? As of 2012, DeLoach had opened her own event planning business, dubbed Sweet Bee.

FUN FACT: Pearl Jam later wrote a song, "Bee Girl," in tribute to the young dancer.

Behind the Music

VH1's *Behind the Music* is the juiciest of TV guilty pleasures. Watching an episode is like flipping through Mom's yearbook and having her explain that the star quarterback got the prom queen pregnant and later both ended up on crack. It zeroes in like Laser Floyd on those once-famous bands who soared close to the sun, then tumbled headfirst into vats of drugs and booze. In other words, all of them.

There's always a bad guy, whether it's the pig farmer turned band manager, the megalomaniacal second wife, or the drummer who can't lift his nose out of the coke mountain. The hits come, and just as quickly stop, while the tragedies pile up like 45s on a turntable.

How did so many of these bands follow the same messed-up paths? Did they all run into each other at rehab, or bankruptcy court? Whatever the reason, the show was a soothing hour full of smugness for viewers. We may not have had a string of number-one R & B hits in 1975, but we also never threw away millions of dollars on sub sandwich franchises and polo ponies.

STATUS: The show shows no sign of ending after fifteen years. As long as there are bands, there will always be bands that get themselves into trouble.

FUN FACT: *The Simpsons* dead-on spoof, *Behind the Laughter*, even borrowed *Behind the Music*'s actual narrator, Jim Forbes. "I had no business hosting the Oscars," explains a confession-minded Lisa. "Meryl Streep spit on me!"

The Big Lebowski

Poor Jeffrey "The Dude" Lebowski. Man didn't want much from life: Nights spent bowling with Donny and Walter. Time to relax in the bathtub without a ferret being dumped on top of him. And most of all, a rug that tied the whole room together.

But that was not to be. Mistaken for a millionaire also named Lebowski, our Los Angeles stoner, hero of Joel and Ethan Coen's *The Big Lebowski*, finds himself caught up in a world of German Nihilists, vaginal art, a car-thieving schoolkid, and a laid-back cowboy narrator.

Robe and jelly shoes on, White Russian in hand, he bobs and weaves through the plot, just trying to get back his simple life. Toes are amputated, Creedence is stolen, but through it all, The Dude abides. We don't know about you, but we take comfort in that.

STATUS: Released in 1998, the film found a new cult following in later years, and a traveling Lebowski Fest now celebrates it annually.

FUN FACT: The Coen Brothers were well aware that it was a ferret, not a marmot, thrown into The Dude's bathtub, but figured the character himself would get the two species mixed up.

Big Mouth Billy Bass

It was the worst thing to happen to mankind's relationship with sea life since Jaws ate all those people. Part robot, part wall art, all bad idea, Big Mouth Billy Bass looked like a stuffed fish mounted on a plaque, but all it took was a quick press of the red button—or, God forbid, doing anything to trip his motion sensor—and battery-powered annoyance kicked in.

A staple of rec rooms everywhere, he'd launch into "Take Me to the River" or "Don't Worry, Be Happy," complete with fish choreography, his little mouth flapping along with the music. Even with his big surprise move (he bent in the middle and did a ninety-degree turn halfway through to stare at you with those dead fish eyes), Billy quickly outstayed his welcome. People all over the world prayed for the sweet relief of dead double-As as they suddenly realized they were severely allergic to rubber seafood.

STATUS: Mercifully, gone for good, although you can still find Billy online and at garage sales everywhere. Before the trend started to smell, it also took the form of a singing lobster, a deer head, and even a fish skeleton.

FUN FACT: Knockoffs and variations included a toy truck draped with a deer carcass that woke up and sang along with the hunters that shot it.

Bill Nye the Science Guy

In the '90s, *Bill Nye the Science Guy* helped more than a few middle schoolers limp through science class. The PBS show, which ran from 1993–1998, tackled everything from eyeballs to evolution, lifting normally dry topics out of textbooks and bringing them to life with a nerdy but fun zing.

Lanky Nye was the science teacher we all wished we had, complete with bow tie and sky-blue lab coat. His show incorporated TV show parodies, James Bond–style scenes, and song spoofs. He dressed in a suit of armor to explain reptile scales and stood in Puget Sound for a lesson on primordial soup. And his techniques actually helped us remember concepts too—in one, he began a bike trip at a red balloon representing the sun, and demonstrated how far it took to reach each of the planets.

Humor, charm, and we were learning too? Man, the best we could hope for from our real teachers was that the pop quiz would get postponed for a day.

STATUS: The show may be gone for good, but Alton Brown's *Good Eats*, which ran from 1999 to 2011, featured a similar nerdy, likable host explaining science-y topics (in this case all related to food) to a general audience. And Nye is still around, blogging and making videos about science.

FUN FACT: A lecture by Nye inspired the creation of the CBS crime show *Numb3rs*, which ran from 2005–2010.

Billy Bob Thornton

Mmm-hmm, Billy Bob Thornton was in movies and TV shows before, but it was in 1996's *Sling Blade*, when he melted into the role of a mentally disabled man who reckons he likes them French-fried potaters, that we all took notice. And got more than a little weirded out over just how much Thornton transformed into the murderous but oddly gentle Karl Childers, who called his weapon of choice a Kaiser blade, while some folks call it a sling blade. For a while in the 1990s that line was as popular as the Macarena, and about a million times more menacing.

Thornton wrote, directed, starred in, and won a screenplay Oscar for *Sling Blade*, and quickly became Hollywood's newest "it" guy. He went on to earn acclaim for roles in 1990s hits *Primary Colors* and *A Simple Plan*, among other films, and became known as an offbeat actor with a quiet intelligence and tough-guy persona.

Thornton wasn't your typical heartthrob, but he was soon dating one of the most beautiful and intriguing women in Hollywood—Angelina Jolie. They wed in 2000, and the media erupted with headlines after learning that the two wore each other's blood in vials around their necks. That's something, all right—when your freakiest role is something out of your real life, not the one where you kill Dwight Yoakam with a lawnmower blade.

STATUS: Still makin' movies.

FUN FACT: He comes by "Billy Bob" naturally—William Robert is his name.

The Blair Witch Project

1999's *The Blair Witch Project* is remembered as much for its separate elements as for the film as a whole. The shaky camera work that made some viewers nauseous. A disturbing close-up of Heather's dripping nostril. The "found footage" gimmick, supporting the rumor that these weren't actors but real filmmakers gone missing. The sense that, given willing friends, a camera, and some ornate piles of twigs, you too could have made this movie in the woods near your house.

Thankfully, though, the novelty added up to a really good scare. When Heather, Josh, and Mike realize they're walking in circles and Mike kicks their only map into the river, when Josh discovers that his belongings have been covered in slime, when Heather unwraps a disturbing bundle of hair and teeth—a sense of dread steamed out of those woods that rivaled anything Jason Voorhees could conjure up.

STATUS: The original film is available on DVD, but more important, the "found footage" genre it helped popularize continues to be popular, especially with horror movies.

FUN FACT: The bloody teeth that are supposed to be Josh's were real human teeth provided by a Maryland dentist.

Blossom Fashion

Yes, *Blossom* had a plot—the eponymous character (Mayim Bialik) maneuvered through life with her single musician dad and two brothers, one a recovering addict and one who was a few peas short of a casserole. But no 1990s kid remembers more than a handful of actual storylines from the 1991–1995 show. We were too busy being completely stunned, intrigued, and occasionally blinded by the weird and wacky wardrobes.

Some people are staunch believers that sunflowers should stay in the garden, where they belong. Or that while Grandma's crocheting may be the pride of the nursing home, when she crafts you a lime green sweater, it's probably best to thank her profusely and wear it only on her birthday. But others looked at Blossom and her best pal Six as trendsetters, slamming together funky, creative, eclectic outfits that somehow . . . worked. Blossom's granny dresses, clunky boots, vests, oversized jackets, and—especially—her floppy, flower-bedecked hats influenced a generation of kooky, fiercely independent kids.

Blossom planted the style-setting seeds that let a generation fly its quirky freak flag—even if it was cobbled together out of yellow long underwear, floppy hats, and a skirt made out of neckties. In our opinionation, that's reason enough to induct her into the '90s Fashion Hall of Fame.

STATUS: Gone for good. Although, in 2012, Bialik and TV sibling Joey Lawrence reprised their roles in a commercial for Old Navy. Whoa. Loads of other shows went on to inspire teens' wardrobe choices, from *Gossip Girl* (headbands!) to *Sex and the City* (tutus!).

FUN FACT: In 2009, Bialik got a post-*Blossom* fashion update on the TLC show *What Not to Wear*. The hosts called her real-life style "homeless hippie," and ripped on her "Blossom-ish" clothing choices that included men's shirts, an antique silk kimono, and yes, her actual grandma's sweater.

Blue's Clues

Only the luckiest kids got a real dog when they begged and pleaded. The rest of us got Blue, the neon cerulean puppy from Nickelodeon's *Blue's Clues* who lived with a motley menagerie of other anthropomorphic animals, furniture, and tools and their flesh-and-blood overlord, Steve Burns. No one thought it was odd that Steve heard the saltshaker, side-table drawer, and pail and shovel talking to him? Or that it took him a half hour to solve a mystery that most preschoolers figured out in the first three minutes?

When Steve left the show in

2002, a new dude named Joe moved into the *Blue's Clues* world and the Internet went nuts with rumors that the original host had actually died. That mystery was quickly solved. (Surprise: He was fine. Steve split to pursue a music career.)

We wish that they'd have given some time to the show's real mysteries. Like how Mr. Salt and Mrs. Pepper gave birth to a jar of paprika, or why Steve always wore the exact same light-and-dark-striped green shirt? Or the solution to the biggest whodunit of all: That when Blue left clues all over the floor, it probably meant she needed to go outside.

STATUS: The show stopped production in 2006, but reruns still air on Nick Jr.

FUN FACT: Steve Burns played a murderer on *Homicide: Life on the Street* in 1998—still wearing a striped shirt.

Bob Ross and
The Joy of Painting

You never really intended to watch *The Joy of Painting* with Bob Ross, but maybe it was late at night, or maybe you were stuck at Grandma's and the remote was not within your control. Or face it, maybe you had just settled down on the couch after a night out and were completely baked.

And there was this guy, in jeans and a white man's Afro, speak-

ing in the gentle voice of a pastor, offering up a painting lesson so sparsely shot it may have been filmed in his garage. He murmured the names of the colors, from titanium white to Prussian blue to burnt umber, as if they were his beloved children. And like a good dad, he had complete faith that his audience could do anything he could do, which in this case meant turn a blank canvas into a mountain masterpiece or a seascape in one half-hour show—if they didn't nod off to sleep first. The *New York Times* once called his voice aural Demerol.

Fans learned a little about Ross in the process, including that his mom was his "favorite lady" and that when fishing he "put a Band-Aid on the fish and gave it CPR" before releasing it. Like Mr. Rogers, he seemed unquestionably good at heart—how could anyone painting "happy little trees" be otherwise? For that half hour, you were in the hands of a gentleman, and there was nothing bad in the world.

STATUS: Gone for good. Ross died in 1995. A personality like Ross's can't be replaced, but his memory lives on through reruns and his line of art supplies.

FUN FACT: A *Far Side* cartoon shows a woman watching a Bob Ross–like show who's crushed to death when a real "happy little tree" falls on her house.

Body Glitter

How did you apply your body glitter? A spray? Lotion? Powder? Those Kissing Potion–like roll-on bottles? Really, the question should be: Why did we apply it at all? What was it about 1990s fashion that made us feel we could best accessorize by coating our skin with sticky, messy sparkles, as if we'd first dressed to the nines, and then sat down and rolled all over a kindergarten craft table?

Cosmetics companies indulged us by offering glitter in all scents, colors, and formats. Want to paint it on your nails? Squirt it in your hair? Dab it on your lips? Sweep it on your eyelids? Mostly we just splashed it on anywhere skin was at all exposed, envisioning ourselves to be hip and trendy club kids, instead of preteens who might as well have asked Claire's at the mall to set up a direct-deposit account for our allowance.

You'd roll the glittery blueberry- or strawberry-scented goodness all over your shoulders, chest, and sometimes midriff, envisioning that the sparkle would surely catch Nick Lachey's eye as he stared out into the nosebleed seats at a 98 Degrees concert. In reality, painting the glitter on was the most fun of the whole exercise, and the least fun part was finding the little sparkly speckles for days afterward on your jeans, in your bedsheets, and absolutely everywhere else.

STATUS: Glitter cosmetics are still around, but you're most likely to find sparkles in fingernail polish these days.

FUN FACT: Glitter was so popular in the 1990s that even mega-chain Bath & Body Works had a line of products, Art Stuff, that seemed designed only to showcase glitter.

Bottled Water

Pay for water? When it already comes free out of the tap, the hose, the drinking fountain, even the sky? Our dads found the very concept as horrifying as leaving the lights on when no one's home. In the 1970s or even 1980s, buying water seemed as silly as the old jokes about selling ice to Eskimos, but by the end of the 1990s, it was a billion-dollar industry.

The bottled-water craze made sense in a way. Water is better for you than sugary pop, so who wouldn't feel a bit smug toting a bottle of the clear stuff instead of a Mountain Dew? But the craze brought its own problems—endless water containers clogging up landfills, as well as concerns about BPA, a chemical used in some plastic bottles. And don't forget the cost—the *New York Times* estimated drinking eight glasses of tap water a day costs a consumer $0.49 a year vs. $1,400 for bottled water.

STATUS: Water continues to be a popular carry-with-you beverage, but more and more people are refilling the same container, oftentimes out of the tap. Thankfully, the next evolution in the you're-paying-for-*what*? craze—oxygen bars—has yet to quite take off.

FUN FACT: "Evian" spelled backward is "naïve."

Boy Bands

B oy bands weren't invented in the 1990s—just ask moms who once swooned for the Monkees. But the late '80s and the '90s saw the trend explode, and junior-high lockers and concert promoters were the richer for it.

Whether you grooved to New Edition, Boyz II Men, 'N Sync, 98 Degrees, the Backstreet Boys, or earlier offering New Kids on the Block, the most important part of boy-band fandom was selecting a favorite band member. Every girl knew immediately if she was going to fall for the Cute One ('N Sync's Justin), the Shy One (Backstreet's Kevin), the Bad Boy (NKOTB's Donnie), or the One Who Was Left Over After All Your Friends Already Called Dibs (oftentimes he was the one who quit the band early and immediately flopped at a solo career).

Thanks to teen magazines and TV specials, you soon knew

your favorite's hobbies, dog's name, preferred foods, and of course his astrological sign and how it compared with your own. Your slightly older brother would mock you endlessly for this trivia, but really, he had no ground to stand on, considering he knew the same factoids about his own chosen idol on the Vikings or Red Sox.

Boy banders embraced the clean-cut, cookie-cutter image that made girls swoon. From the meticulously coordinated outfits to the never-out-of-step choreography, this was music cranked out by the corporate machine. But who cared? The harmonies soared, the tunes made for perfect prom themes, and the singers themselves were cuter than Beanie Babies. They had the right stuff, baby.

STATUS: Various bands popular in the 1990s have made comebacks, and in the 2010s, Europe began feeding us new boy bands, with One Direction leading the way.

FUN FACT: New Kids on the Block spawned a short-lived cartoon in 1990–1991. The real band members would appear briefly before the episodes to deliver messages about how much they loved camping or to urge fans to stay in school.

The Brady Bunch Revival

Here's the story . . . of a lovely lady. And her family, who never left our minds.

Campily classic sitcom *The Brady Bunch* was canceled in 1974, but never really ended. Reruns ran eternally, and there also was a cartoon, variety show complete with synchronized swimming, *The Brady Brides* TV series, and *A Very Brady Christmas*.

But it was in the 1990s that the famed blended family came back into the spotlight. *The Real Live Brady Bunch* dramatized scripts onstage. The 1990 drama *The Bradys* brought the family into a more troubled era (Marcia's an alcoholic! Bobby gets paralyzed!). Two big-screen movies parodied the original series. Suddenly, the Bradys, who'd never really been cool, were everywhere.

Many kids who grew up watching the Bradys didn't have the happy family they saw on the show. They sought comfort in it as kids, and as adults, they enjoyed the family reunion. Interest in the Bradys peaked around 1995, but it's never truly gone away. Every generation, it seems, longs to somehow form a family.

STATUS: Members of the *Bunch* keep popping up, and in 2012, Vince Vaughn and CBS were working on yet another reboot of the famous family.

FUN FACT: Stars who made it big after stints on *The Real Live Brady Bunch* include Andy Richter (who played Mike), Jane Lynch (Carol), and Melanie Hutsell (Jan).

Brenda Walsh

Not many TV characters spawn a newsletter and a song devoted to hating them, but Brenda Walsh on Fox's hit *Beverly Hills, 90210* was not your average TV character. Shannen

Doherty's Minnesota twin turned California brat may have had plenty of dates onscreen, but to viewers, she was as unpopular as emergency dental work.

Brenda was a piece of work indeed. She shoplifted. Called best friend Kelly a bimbo. Slapped OHN-drea because they both had a crush on the drama teacher. Ran away from home. Pretended to be French to fool a guy she met in Paris. Blabbed about her friends' flaws to a TV reporter. Her back-and-forth with Kelly and side-burned loner Dylan was a love triangle to rival Edward-Bella-Jacob in its day.

And just as with *Twilight*, fans' feelings about the character leaked over into real life. Doherty's offscreen troubles tied right in with the character's slide from dutiful midwestern daughter to West Beverly bad girl. Brenda was written off the show after its fourth season, with her character ostensibly enrolling at London's Royal Academy of Dramatic Arts, a plotline at least as realistic as when Dylan spent his summer racing motorcycles in Europe and climbing K2.

STATUS: Brenda Walsh returned again, still played by Doherty, on the CW series *90210*, which premiered in 2008. Surprise! She was still fighting with Kelly over Dylan.

FUN FACT: Fans' hatred of the character carried over to actress Doherty, and Darby Romeo of the *Ben Is Dead* zine's *I Hate Brenda Newsletter* rode that zeitgeist. In the newsletter, no less than Eddie Vedder himself dissed the actress.

Bubble Tape

When the Mad Scientists of Gum World get bored, they think of a new shape or container for their stretchy, chewy treat. There are gum Band-Aids, gum lollipops, bubblegum cigars, and the Chewapalooza that delighted '90s kids' mouths, Bubble Tape.

The best thing about Bubble Tape wasn't actually the gum but the circular container, which parceled out gum in long strips like—duh—tape. Even kids from antitobacco homes couldn't resist pretending the round plastic box was a tin of Skoal—though this worked better after you'd chewed all the Bubble Tape and refilled it with shredded Big League Chew.

The gum itself was a tightly rolled snail of flat, sweet heaven, testing kids in the one area where they had no self-discipline— portion control. Sure the prim goody-goody in social studies could

probably break off a tiny slice and make it last till study hall, but the rest of us crammed at least four of the promised six feet of gum into our mouths at once.

STATUS: Still around.

FUN FACT: At Christmas time, there's a seasonal candy-cane flavor, but what kid likes mint gum?

Buffy the Vampire Slayer

Before the sparkly vampires of *Twilight* and the studly naked ones of HBO's *True Blood*, the most fashionable fanged folk were the craggy-faced undead who fed on the denizens of Sunnydale.

Luckily, Buffy the Vampire Slayer was there to turn them to dust—while skewering 'em with sharper-than-a-stake one-liners.

Five years after the terrible 1992 movie, creator Joss Whedon got it oh so right and constructed a television world full of demons and heroes, filled with both sweeping themes and teeny-tiny moments. Buffy, watcher Giles, witch-in-training Willow, regular guy Xander, popular girl Cordelia, demon Anya, werewolf Oz, and hey-where'd-you-come-from? sister Dawn, not to mention (sometimes) reformed vamps Angel and Spike, saved the world. A lot. And all while Buffy maneuvered through universal high school woes like homework and finding a date that wouldn't try to drag her into the Hellmouth.

A little like Buffy herself, the UPN/WB show looked harmless and frivolous on its surface but it had a smart, deep soul. It was always surprising: The nearly silent episode spoke volumes. The musical episode sparked a decade of me-too singing-and-dancing episodes from other shows (really, *Grey's Anatomy*, really?). And the heartbreaking episode where Buffy's mother suddenly died— not at the hands of a demon, but from an aneurysm—was as powerful as anything on TV. Ever. No wonder *Buffy* made *Time* magazine's list of the one hundred best TV shows of all time. It was bloody good.

STATUS: Buffy slayed her last vamp in 2003, but the tales continued in comic-book form. Spinoff *Angel* lasted until 2004. Creator Whedon shed his cult status in a spectacular way in 2012 when he wrote and directed *The Avengers*, the third-highest-grossing movie of all time.

FUN FACT: Before he was Giles, Anthony Stewart Head starred in those flirty, soap-opera-y Taster's Choice commercials that ran in the mid-'90s.

Bungee Jumping

How did bungee jumping ever get popular? Shouldn't we be paying people big money to help us *not* fall off a scarily high surface? Still, this sport/suicide method became a weekend activity to rival horseback riding or roller skating for some '90s daredevils.

Why did people throw themselves off a high bridge with just a rubbery cord attached to their foot? For the same flood of adrenaline that made some people skydive or parasail, or drive into downtown Chicago at rush hour. Those of us who'd rather tease rabid wolverines than bungee had our beliefs reinforced by watching the nightly news, which gleefully covered the trend whenever somebody misjudged and head met pavement.

By the 2000s, bungee jumping was a regular component of shows like *The Amazing Race* or *Fear Factor*. It also became a thrill ride at state fairs, because after stuffing down a corn dog, chocolate malt, cheese curds, and some deep-fried pickles, the best thing for your already-roiling stomach was a barf-inducing leap from a high distance. You knew you'd see those pickles again anyway, didn't you?

STATUS: Daredevils still do it.

FUN FACT: In 1995, at the height of the craze, super spy James Bond bungee jumps to escape an enemy in the opening of *GoldenEye*. He ended up both shaken and stirred.

Caboodles

They looked like Dad's fishing tackle box, except Fleet Farm didn't sell tackle boxes in hot pink with aqua and lavender accents. Caboodles were makeup cases for girls who really weren't old enough to wear makeup. So your three-level Caboodle might hold four Chapsticks, one Great Lash mascara on the verge of drying out, some Avon perfume samples from the next-door neighbor's garage sale, totally stylin' ribbon barrettes, and Mom's shocking turquoise eye shadow that would have been a favorite of Mimi from *The Drew Carey Show*.

Of course you had to haul your Caboodle to your best friend's house for a sleepover, and she'd bring hers out too. You'd swap products and organize as if you were surgeons preparing tools for a

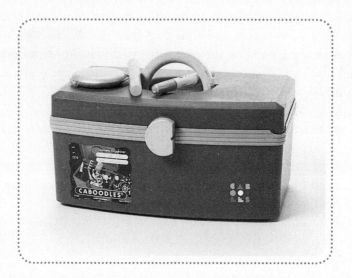

heart transplant, not middle schoolers who weren't allowed to wear makeup to school anyway. Like Barbie's pink Corvette, Caboodles were less about who you were and more about the image of who you might someday become. They were plastic pastel dream academies with removable segments.

STATUS: They're still available, sleeker and more stylish than the originals.

FUN FACT: The first-ever Caboodle was pink, and was created in 1987. The idea was inspired by a 1986 *People* magazine photo of Vanna White using a tackle box to store her makeup.

Caller ID and Star-69

Before the crazy phone innovations of the 1990s, the telephone's role was simple and straightforward. You dialed. It rang. Or it rang, you picked up.

But then came caller ID, which identified who was calling before you even answered, and then the last-call-return function known as star-69. It was like we were living with the Jetsons. Oh my God, it's *him* calling! Or maybe, Ewww, it's him calling. With caller ID, the caller's name and number were right there glowing at you. Still mad at your lab partner? Ignore her call with your head held high! Don't want to go bring the phone to your brother just so he can yack with his baseball buddy? Strike three for him—don't answer that call!

Using star-69 to identify a missed call was great when you came racing into the house just as that final ring was dying away, but it did put a bit of a damper on every girl's favorite hobby of calling your crush repeatedly just to panic and hang up.

We'd barely become accustomed to phone calls losing their anonymity when cell phones made these innovations obsolete. Now your smart phone automatically pops up the number, and often the name, of whoever's calling you, and we don't give it a second thought. Sure, you can avoid solicitors and nagging relatives, but an element of mystery got lost along the way.

STATUS: Caller I-what? Star sixty-who? The next generation has all but ditched phone calls in favor of texting anyway.

FUN FACT: In the movie-inside-the-movie in 1997's *Scream 2*, when Heather Graham receives a phone call from the unknown killer, Jada Pinkett yells at her to "Hang up and star-69 his ass!"

Calvin and Hobbes

There had been mischievous kids in the comics before (*Dennis the Menace, Family Circus*). There'd also been anthropomorphic animals (Snoopy, Garfield). But never was there a combination like the little boy and stuffed tiger of *Calvin and Hobbes*, which ran from 1985 to 1995.

Calvin was an unstoppable little force of nature in a striped shirt, and with Hobbes by his side, he could do anything. He built terrifying snowmen, including a batch that were vomiting in protest of his mom's eggplant casserole. He invented Calvinball, a random prop-filled game with ever-changing rules and final scores such as "Q to 12." He tormented his parents, teachers, and babysitters, and formed GROSS—the Get Rid Of Slimy girlS club—to agonize little Susie Derkins.

Calvin was driven by an axis of little-boy chutzpah and an imagination that knew no bounds. A cardboard box became a Transmogrifier, turning him into a mini version of Hobbes. A game of doctor ended in a fight when Susie resists Dr. Calvin's prescription of a lobotomy for her minor foot injury. When crabby teacher Miss Wormwood asked Calvin what state he lives in, he happily replied, "Denial," and there was really no reason to argue with that.

There was a purity to *Calvin and Hobbes* that few other comic strips ever found. Artist Bill Watterson resisted licensing his creation, not that this prevented every car enthusiast on the planet from snatching up a bootleg bumper sticker of Calvin peeing on the logo of a competitor. But when Watterson closed the door on Calvin's world in 1995, he went out as far up on top as a comic strip could. Off sailed Calvin and Hobbes on their sled, leaving behind a world that felt a little less magical, and a newspaper comics page that never quite recovered.

STATUS: Gone for good. No strip has truly replaced *Calvin and Hobbes* in readers' hearts.

FUN FACT: "Derkins," the last name of Calvin's nemesis, Susie, was the name of Watterson's wife's family beagle.

Cassette Tapes

The music format of one's childhood never lasts. Vinyl albums are now a novelty, 8-tracks a punch line, and CDs are getting their butts kicked digitally by iTunes. But let us stop and say a prayer of thanks for the elegant cassette tape, which for a quarter of a century wrapped its magical magnetic ribbons around our music-loving hearts.

Tapes were smaller and sleeker than 8-tracks, and they fit nicely in the shoeboxes we stacked in closets and under our beds. But the best thing about them was the DIY aspect. You could make your own recordings so easily, whether you were taping the *Rugrats* soundtrack off the TV with your Fisher-Price tape recorder or creating your own monster movie with a hand-scribbled script and a batch of squirmy cousins. And of course, our favorite thing to do with cassettes was to make mix tapes, for ourselves and for friends.

Professional musicians working on multimillion-dollar albums couldn't have fussed more about the order and song choice than we did, sprawled in our bedroom with a blank see-through TDK tape and a double-sided boom box. Would the boy of our dreams make the connection between "Friday I'm in Love" and the fact that we had identical class schedules on Fridays? Was "Kiss from a Rose" too forward, "Wonderwall" too subtle? Would the ex-boyfriend we pined for pick up the hint we were dropping with "Your Wildest Dreams"? When the music plays, would he hear the sound he had to follow?

Cassettes had their problems. We grew to be experts at rewinding a tangled tape by sticking a ballpoint pen or a pencil in one of the reel holes. Like the romances they helped us nurture, tapes had short lifespans, always seeming to break at the worst possible moment. But as the 1990s ended and CDs rolled in, it was hard not to hold on to those cassette-crammed shoeboxes much longer than we should have. We just weren't ready to hit eject on our musical memories.

STATUS: Tapes will never be as popular as they once were, but a loyal contingent still loves them. In 2010, NPR reported that at least twenty-five music labels were still stubbornly distributing music on tapes.

FUN FACT: In 2011, the phrase "cassette tape" was removed from the concise version of the Oxford English Dictionary. One of the words it made room for? "Sexting."

Celebrity Movies

Was there some sort of terrible-movie-loving genie granting wishes to athletes, wrestlers, and rappers in the '90s? How else do you explain that fact that nearly every nonacting celebrity was given a chance to nonact in his own movie?

Someone thought it was a good plan to cast jock Brian Bosworth as a cop who played by his own rules in 1991's *Stone Cold*. The *Washington Post* said it perfectly: "Carl Weathers and Dolph Lundgren are both Shakespearean actors compared with Bosworth." Singer Vanilla Ice eyeballed that incredibly low cinematic bar and sailed right underneath it as a motorcycle-riding rapper who played by his own rules in *Cool as Ice*. Stop, collaborate, and listen: Whoever's idea that was, you're fired.

For some reason, people kept giving wrestler Hulk Hogan second, third, and fourth chances to become a movie star, with terrible flicks like *Suburban Commando*, *Mr. Nanny*, and one of the worst movies ever made, *Santa with Muscles*. In that 1996 disaster, the Hulkster played a millionaire with amnesia who thought he was Kris Kringle. Naturally, he wore studded black-leather gloves with his Santa suit, as you would.

Basketball star Dennis Rodman and his multicolored hair starred in a couple of duds as well: *Double Team* and *Simon Sez*. Simon says: Rodman, Hogan, and everybody else with little natural acting talent, please stop making movies.

STATUS: Still popular, and now more female nonactors are getting their big-screen shots too. Witness: Christina Aguilera in 2010's *Burlesque* or Miley Cyrus in anything.

FUN FACT: *Cool as Ice* debuted at a rock-bottom number fourteen the week it opened, an embarrassing nine places below *Scared Stupid*, starring Ernest.

Cheetos Paws

C heetos have come in puffs and twists, balls and whirls, but none of the brand's long-lost junk-food variants are as much missed as a 1991 marvel known as Cheetos Paws.

In the commercials, hepcat snacking mascot Chester Cheetah would hand the treat out to boys and girls on the playground like a furry crack dealer. The kids would go so nuts for the puffy orange pillows, and for good reason: Paws were extra-fluffy and thick, and more aerodynamic than the caveman-club-shaped regular Cheetos.

But why wasn't anybody getting bent out of shape over what should have been the biggest snack-food scandal of the '90s—the fact that Chester Cheetah was selling his own severed hands to hungry children?

STATUS: Frito-Lay keeps cranking out the new flavors and shapes, but so far no other bags of cheetah body parts.

FUN FACT: In Japan, Cheetos come in such flavors as strawberry, chocolate, and wasabi-mayonnaise.

Clarissa Explains It All

Before she played a teenage witch, Melissa Joan Hart was the confident and spunky title character with funky fashion sense and a heck of an imagination on *Clarissa Explains It All*. The show, which ran from 1991–1994 on Nickelodeon, broke new ground as it broke the fourth wall: Clarissa talked directly to the viewer as she deftly dealt with such problems as boys, pimples, and her annoying redheaded brother, Ferguson.

The mini–Mary Tyler Moore had a slew of boyfriends throughout the show's four-year run, but the one dude who stood by her through it all was her platonic guy-pal Sam. Although why in the world were Clarissa's parents okay with the stalker-like way he always visited: on a ladder through a second-story window?

Clarissa was an all-American girl, but with a decidedly adult side, quoting Karl Marx, actually saying the word "sex," and getting arrested for protesting animal testing. Wonder if it had something to do with show writer Suzanne Collins, who went on to create the kajillion-selling, not-for-little-kids phenomenon *The Hunger Games*. Wouldn't it have been awesome if Clarissa would have stalked Ferg-face with a bow and arrow, Katniss-style? Clarissa would have had a lot of explaining to do.

STATUS: Clarissa's grrrl power inspired other teen shows like *iCarly* and *The Secret World of Alex Mack*. As of 2013, Nickelodeon was re-airing this and other classic '90s shows.

FUN FACT: In 2008, Denver band L'elan Vital released a song called "Clarissa Didn't Explain Shit."

Clear Colas

If the colors of the 1970s were earthy tones like harvest gold and avocado green, and the colors of the 1980s were the sunshiny pastels of *Miami Vice*, what was left for the 1990s? For a while in the early part of the decade, marketers just gave up on color completely, and suddenly, clear was the way to go.

Clear sodas, including Tab Clear and Clearly Canadian. Miller

Clear beer and the much-derided Zima. Clear soaps. Even clear trash bags were introduced—because if there's one thing you want to get a good sharp look at, it's a mashed-up bunch of garbage.

Crystal Pepsi, a caffeine-free beverage introduced with a Super Bowl ad featuring Van Halen's hit song "Right Now," led the see-through cola pack in late 1992 and early 1993. But gone along with the color? The flavor. Once the big publicity push died down, consumers couldn't see their way clear to keep buying the nasty stuff, and a reformulated citrus version went sour almost instantly.

STATUS: Gone for good, but a drink called Pepsi Clear was briefly sold in Mexico in 2005.

FUN FACT: The best surviving artifact of the clear cola craze? *Saturday Night Live*'s hilarious Crystal Gravy commercial parody, which featured Kevin Nealon splashing the clear goo on his face in the shower and Julia Sweeney dipping a chicken leg into a jar of the stuff.

Clerks

Kevin Smith's success was the American dream. Scrounging up money through credit cards, a parental loan, and the sale of his comic-book collection, this regular Joe from New Jersey made *Clerks* for $27,000 in 1994 and raked in millions—and began an enviable directorial career.

Things weren't quite so rosy for his characters. Dante fended off shoplifters, egg examiners, and an antismoking gum rep, and also discovered that his girlfriend was a total nympho. Pal Randal in the neighboring video store actively tried to chase away customers, reading a list of porn titles in front of a mom and daughter and recommending the worst movies he can think of. (*Smokey and the Bandit 3*, anyone?)

Clerks earned acclaim for its witty script, which was so layered with profanities that it almost received an NC-17 status. The movie raters at the MPAA may not have understood, but a generation of minimum-wage workers found kindred spirits in the clock-punching slackers they saw onscreen. As he said over and over again in the film, Dante wasn't even supposed to be there that day, but thank Hollywood and a chubby comic-book geek from Jersey that he was.

STATUS: *Clerks II* came out in 2006. Lord, it was terrible.

FUN FACT: Smith's original script ended with Dante being shot to death by a robber.

"Closing Time"

Closing time—one last call for alcohol, so finish your whiskey or beer." When the lights came up in any late-'90s bar at the end of the night, it was a near certainty you'd hear this ubiquitous Semisonic song. Millions of drunks gathered up their jackets and moved it to the exits to the bouncy strains of the familiar tune. Even today, whenever some people hear it on the radio, they swear they smell stale Schlitz.

Unlike most '90s tunes, "Closing Time" persisted, wrapping its catchy tendrils around pop culture. It's a recurring joke in the Justin Timberlake–Mila Kunis flick *Friends with Benefits* (Timberlake thinks it's by Third Eye Blind). Danny McBride beats up Robert Downey Jr. and Zach Galifianakas to it in *Due Date*. And Jennifer Egan referenced it in her 2011 Pulitzer Prize–winning book *A Visit from the Goon Squad*.

But few realized it wasn't just a literal ode to the end of the night. According to Semisonic's Dan Wilson, who wrote the song, it was also a metaphor for being born. ("Time for you to go back to the places you will be from.") Whoa—deep. And lost on most of the people stumbling out of a bar to barf into a snowbank.

STATUS: "Closing Time" continues to trump other popular end-of-night tunes, including "Happy Trails" by Gene Autry and 50 Cent's "Get Out Da Club."

FUN FACT: The final episode of *Melrose Place* featured "Closing Time" just before the credits rolled.

Coke MagiCan Promotion

Amerdica near the end of the twentieth century had the best contests. Publisher's Clearing House, where people win a fake check the size of a pool table. McDonald's Monopoly, which was just as drawn-out and unwinnable as the real thing. And for a brief shining moment in 1990, the Coke MagiCan contest.

MagiCan was that rare game where companies actually messed with their own product. You may have thought you were getting a can of Coke, but if you were a winner, your Coke can was filled not with soda, but weird-tasting and specially stinkified chlorinated water. The can also featured a spring-loaded device that popped up your prize—maybe a five-dollar bill, maybe a coupon for cash or prizes that you had to take to a nearby Coke bottler to redeem.

Of course, we kids tried to game the system, shaking each can on the store shelf and listening to see if it offered any clues about what was sloshing around inside. And then leaving them on the shelf and going on our merry way, a happy little splashy surprise for the next unsuspecting consumer.

STATUS: The contest didn't make it past 1990.

FUN FACT: Some MagiCans jammed, some leaked, and one eleven-year-old kid got sick from drinking the yucky water in a malfunctioning can.

COPS

COPS hit the ground running after its first suspect in 1989 and hasn't pulled over since. The Fox reality show taught us that police officers aren't always knee-deep in a Hollywood-style murder investigation—most of the time they're out pounding the beat, breathalyzing drunks, separating angry neighbors, and filling out thrilling paperwork.

Best of all are the chases, of course, whether seen from a squad car-mounted camera or from the jostling view of a *COPS* cameraman, who earns his pay and then some just for keeping up with the fleeing suspects. And of course, it's sweet schadenfreude to see just how dim criminals can be. Highlights include the guy who tried to flee a fast-food robbery in light-up tennis shoes, the Einstein who tried to eat a bag of pot, and the multitude of citizens who choose to drive completely naked.

Deserving of special mention is *COPS'* uber-catchy theme song. Bad boys, bad boys, whatcha gonna do? When the Shub Jub Shun come foh you! Wait, it's actually "When Sheriff John Brown come for you?" Okay. If you say so, officer.

STATUS: Still on the air.

FUN FACT: The line "I've got him at gunpoint, Thirty-two and Bush," heard over the show's closing credits, refers to a Portland, Oregon, address on Bush Street.

Cuba Gooding Jr.

Sure, winners of the Best Supporting Actor Oscar don't always exactly become household names. Isn't that right, Dean Jagger, Melvyn Douglas, and Joseph Schildkraut? But we were expecting big things from Cuba Gooding Jr. after he took home the little gold statue for his energetic, likable performance as football star Rod Tidwell in 1996's *Jerry Maguire*. Heck, the actor even outshined Tom Cruise and his megawatt smile and adorable moppet Jonathan Lipnicki ("A human head weighs eight pounds"), who was apparently created by mad scientists in a cuteness lab.

And then *Boat Trip* happened. Okay, in all fairness, Gooding made a string of dubious career decisions before he starred with Horatio Sanz in that 2002 stinkfest of a movie, which made everyone who saw it seasick. How bad was it? Gooding dresses in a metallic peacock outfit and later throws up on Vivica A. Fox. And those were the two best scenes in the movie.

STATUS: Cuba has bounced back with roles in less embarrassing fare like *American Gangster*, *Radio*, and *Red Tails*. But come on, Cuba. You're better than *Land Before Time XIII*. Show me the money, indeed.

FUN FACT: Gooding's father (and namesake) was the lead singer of the R & B group the Main Ingredient, which had a hit in 1972 with the song "Everybody Plays the Fool."

Dawson's Creek

You know the Paula Cole–sung theme song: "I don't wanna wait . . . for *Buffy the Vampire Slayer* to be oh-ver, so I can watch *Dawson's Creek* on the WB . . ." Well, we think it went something like that. We do know that in the late 1990s, TV-watching teens were transported weekly to the fictional seaside town of Capeside, Massachusetts, home of Dawson, Joey, Pacey, and Jen, and their *Falcon Crest*–meets–*Saved by the Bell* lives.

The show made teen idols out of its stars, and helped kick off the WB as a network, plus created a new national craze for angst-filled teen shows. You'd be angsty too if, like Dawson, you had a forehead so large fans dubbed it a "fivehead," or if, like Joey and Pacey, you had names that might have sounded better on kangaroos or racehorses. But *Dawson's* devotees didn't care. They were sucked in by the undeniable charm of the lead actors, the ever-changing romances, and the engaging and witty dialogue. Sure, no one we knew talked as wordily as these kids, but then no one we knew had an affair with their English teacher or platonically slept in the same bed with the beautiful girl next door either.

For kids who grew up right along with the *Dawson's* four, the 2003 finale was a monumental event. A little sorrow (Jen dies!), a little romance (Joey chooses Pacey!), and a little wish fulfillment (Dawson meets Steven Spielberg!). The show's themes were hard to resist. Everyone can relate to the irresistible pull of home and the comfort and the confidence of childhood friends turned adults— even those of us who didn't have our own creeks.

STATUS: Gone for good, except for DVDs and reruns. It's been replaced by scores of angsty-teen shows, from *The O.C.* to *One Tree Hill*.

FUN FACT: Katie Holmes's Joey, not James Van Der Beek's Dawson, was the only character to appear in every episode.

Department 56

T hink you're too old for a dollhouse once you actually have a mortgage on a real house? Think again. Thanks to Department 56 and its dozens of little ceramic houses, millions of collectors never had to outgrow their hobby.

Department 56 cranked out its first six buildings in 1976 and never looked back. Crafty moms (this was rarely a hobby for dads) chose one or more of the company's many series and started collecting the little light-up churches, homes, and businesses the way their kids collected baseball cards. The villages were almost all Christmas–themed, but once you had them installed on your bookshelves or end tables, they pretty much stayed out all year.

The buildings themselves might have sprung straight from a Thomas Kinkade painting. Quaintness and charm ruled, with the modern world only a distant memory (although there is a McDonald's, it's an old-fashioned one).

The ultimate frustration for kids? The delicate accessories would shatter like frozen taffy if you were at all clumsy. So while it might look irresistible to race those little ice skaters, put the dog in the mailbox, or see if the caroling nuns could balance on the church roof, your messing around was bound to end in tears and a dustpan full of razor-sharp shards.

STATUS: New houses come out each year.

FUN FACT: Department 56 began as a part of Bachman's, a Minneapolis florist, and took its name from the fact that the store's wholesale gift-import division was its fifty-sixth department.

Dippin' Dots

Just when ice cream seemed like it was a pretty mature technology, along came the sci-fi snackable known as Dippin' Dots, ice cream frozen in liquid nitrogen and served up in little dishes of colorful, edible beads. Found at state fair booths and in some malls, it was a science experiment from the gods.

Who the heck invented this stuff, George Jetson? (Actually, it was microbiologist Curt Jones.) It looked like something that would pop out of the *Star Trek* food replicator. We didn't actually realize you could freeze ice cream any more than it was already frozen, but there was always something loopy and fun about savoring a dish of Dots. You shoveled in a spoonful and your mouth took it from there, melting and squashing the dots together and carpeting your tongue with cold. You could pretend you were eating food pills from the future, or that you were an astronaut sampling interplanetary cuisine.

Their slogan, the "Ice Cream of the Future," always seemed a little odd to us, though. As futuristic as the treat seemed, how could we be eating the ice cream of the future here in the present? And if we had Dippin' Dots yesterday, didn't that make them the ice cream of our fairly recent past? Our advice: Try not to think about it, and just get us a spoon.

STATUS: New owners took over in 2012, and the tasty treats are still fixtures at fairs and malls.

FUN FACT: A Dippin' Dots Frozen Dot Maker lets you cook up a version of the treat at home, but actual liquid nitrogen does not seem to be involved.

Discovery Zone

Forget the mind-numbing bleep-bloop of arcades. At indoor play-center chain Discovery Zone, kids got to run, slide, and jump like the little wild animals they were, burning calories and blasting boredom along the way. Who can forget that first-ever jump into a ball pit, swimming through the brightly colored circles like a happy gumball? Or crawling across the marshmallowy mats that were nothing like the rock-hard versions we knew from gym class? You could swing on trapezes, leap in bounce houses, or chase your little sister through different maze levels like mutant hamsters in a Habitrail.

Discovery Zone let imaginative kids write their own mental

screenplays that they'd then enlist friends to help carry out. Okay, we're moon explorers, and now we're diving into a crater! Or: There's a pirate treasure chest buried in this ball pit, and the first person to dive to the bottom gets it! DZ was a crazily creative, gigantic jungle gym, and for a certain segment of 1990s kids, it seems as if every friend you had hosted their birthday party there.

Of course, it was too good to last. Founded in 1990, the chain filed for bankruptcy mid-decade, and many locations were bought by Chuck E. Cheese, the pizza parlor arcade chain. Is it any wonder that America has a child obesity epidemic? RIP, DZ.

STATUS: It's gone, but elements of Discovery Zone live on in places like McDonald's PlayPlace, Gymboree, certain pizza parlors, and various arcades.

FUN FACT: An early slogan promised "Funbelievable fitness for kids!"

"Don't Copy That Floppy!"

The two kid stars of this classic anti-piracy video appear to have never seen a computer before in their lives, simply mashing their hands randomly down on its keyboard. When they attempt to copy a game, MC Double Def DP, the whitest black rapper ever, delivers a cringeworthy rap about the evils of piracy, name-checking classic games such as *The Oregon Trail* and *Tetris*, all apparently while suffering a shoulder seizure.

To send the video over the top, the rap pauses to let nerdy pro-grammers drone on about their jobs, then finishes up with the kind of special effects that used to exist only on AOL home pages with dancing hamsters. We're pretty sure that for a background, the cameraman just propped up a Lisa Frank folder.

In the end, the kids decide to pay for the game, since then it will come with a manual. Because that's what kids of the '90s really wanted, an unreadable, jargon-filled, phone-book-sized computer game manual. Wrote a commenter on YouTube: "Well, I guess it worked. No one is copying floppies anymore."

STATUS: In 2009, "Don't Copy That 2" was released, in which teens laugh at the original video and learn about how software pirates can go to jail. Also, there are Klingons.

FUN FACT: M. E. Hart, the actor who plays MC Double Def DP in the video, has a degree in Russian language and a law degree. Nyet!

Doritos 3D

Imagine how excited the food scientists at Frito-Lay must have been when they invented Doritos 3D in 1997, giving each other orange-fingered high-fives and relieved that they finally had a three-dimensional snack to rub in the faces of their Planters Cheez Ball-hawking competitors.

The snacks were a little Bugle-y, but instead of being horn-shaped, these were puffy pillows of corn that resembled rounded triangles with a bad case of gas. You'd crunch into them, hit the hollow center, and then chomp through the other side. It was like biting into a Christmas ornament, only with shards of zesty ranch-flavored glass. Some of us gobbled them plain. Some of us dipped. Some of us cracked the little guys open and filled them with squirt cheese. And all of us, whether we'll admit it or not, tossed, flicked, or chucked the fat little footballs across the room.

They were so fragile, if you tried to keep a few in your back-pack or pocket, all you were left with was a pile of Dorito dust. So when they broke open, where did all that Dorito-scented air go? Our guess is it escaped into the atmosphere and now surrounds the Earth, protecting us like a jalapeno-cheddar-scented ozone layer.

STATUS: They disappeared in the 2000s, but serious snackers aren't letting them go without a fight. A "Bring Back Doritos 3D!" Facebook page has thousands of fans.

FUN FACT: In 2001, to coincide with the release of Disney/Pixar's *Monsters, Inc.*, Frito-Lay launched "Monster Colorz" Doritos 3Ds, which turned your mouth blue.

Dream Phone Game

What the Mystery Date board game was to an earlier generation, Dream Phone was to 1990s girls. Mystery Date featured a dorky plastic door that opened to reveal your date for the evening, but Dream Phone added technology, centering around a battery-powered hot pink cordless phone. Players found a photo card with the boy of their choice and punched in his phone number, and a geeky voice delivered a private clue as to which boy had a crush on you. Players recorded clues on a scorecard and when ready to make a guess, called the boy they suspected to learn if they were right.

All the little Dream Phone details added up to a major gigglefest.

Some of the guys on the cards were cute (Dave! Call me!) but others looked like psycho killers (Steve!), nerdy little brothers (Phil!), or your 'roid-raging neighbor who wore nothing but Zubaz (Carlos!). What was up with Tony's earring, Mark's rainbow shirt, John's dorky suspenders, and just how many layers of sweatshirts was Dan wearing? (We count four.) The clues were equally hilarious. "He'll eat anything, except hot dogs." Well, then he really won't eat *anything*, now, *will he*?

At an age when calling a real boy was as unimaginable as going to the moon, Dream Phone let us practice for that far-off day by boldly punching up a number while our pals cheered us on. We would hold one-sided conversations Milton Bradley never dreamed of, suggesting Bob pluck his eyebrows or dissolving in hysterics at George's uneven dye job. And when you finally heard those magic words: "You're right! I really like you!" it was impossible not to shout out with glee and diss your undateable friends. Wrong number for you, suckahs!

STATUS: The latest Dream Phone edition replaces the enormous hot pink handset with a smartphone and delivers clues via text message.

FUN FACT: The game's instructions warn you that the included instrument is "not a real phone."

Dunkaroos

Kids are trained early to dip their snacks. If it's not potato chips in onion dip, or tortilla chips in salsa, it's otherwise healthy vegetables in diet-destroying ranch dressing or McNuggets in sweet and sour sauce.

So in 1988, Kid Snack World was perfectly primed for Betty Crocker's Dunkaroos, kangaroo-shaped cookies that came with a tiny swimming pool of frosting. You sent your tasty Aussie friend off the high dive and into a calorie-laden bath of sweet, sweet icing, then barely let him have a second to shake off the excess before rebounding him smack into Lake Mouth. A later Cookies 'n Creme version let kids build and overstuff their own sandwich cookies, Double Stuf Oreo-style.

Although invented in the 1980s, Dunkaroos might be the

most 1990s snack there was. It's easy to find a nineties kid with fond memories of wolfing these down in front of ABC's TGIF block, with a six-pack of Crystal Pepsi at hand to wash them down.

STATUS: Dunkaroos are hard to find these days, and many fans mistakenly think they've been discontinued. Try Walmart, Costco, your local dollar store, or order online from Amazon.

FUN FACT: The original mascot was an Australian kangaroo named Sydney, but for some reason, Betty Crocker decided to hold a contest and replaced him with Duncan, a new 'roo with an American voice, a backward baseball cap, and a love of daredevil stunts.

Earring Magic Ken

Poor Ken could never compete with the glamour and glitz of girlfriend Barbie. Mattel was so determined to ensure he was nonthreatening that they went over the edge and made him just plain goofy, encouraging Barbie to zoom off in her hot pink Corvette with GI Joe or the Six Million Dollar Man doll instead. And then, in 1993 . . . Earring Magic Ken.

Mattel surveyed girls to determine if Barbie should get a new boyfriend, and the little ladies said no, but that really, Ken should look a little cooler. The toy giant somehow translated "cooler" to equal "Castro District resident circa 1988." Earring Magic Ken featured two-tone hair, a pierced ear, purple mesh shirt, shiny lilac

vest, and, weirdly, a circular necklace that commentators such as Dan Savage instantly declared to be uh, an intimate pleasure device.

This Ken was all set to perform a rousing chorus of "Y-M-C-A!" or take in the latest Liza Minnelli theater show, but he was perhaps unlikely to be interested in hitting the prom with Barbie. The doll quickly became a hot collectible with gay men, while the toy company quietly discontinued him.

STATUS: It's actually hard to find a Ken that can't be misinterpreted. 1996's Big Brother Ken comes with his own toddler boy, 1999's Shave N Style Ken carries a man purse, and let's not even mention Hot Skatin' Ken.

FUN FACT: In 2010's *Toy Story 3*, Ken's girly handwriting and closet full of flashy outfits are the subject of more than one joke at his expense. Not that there's anything wrong with that.

Ebola Virus

What kid didn't crank up the sniffles, fake a fever, and tell their parents they couldn't go to school because they were pretty sure they had the Ebola virus? And why wouldn't they? In the '90s the exotic illness was everywhere, thanks in large part to Richard Preston's horrifying—and all too true—bestselling book, *The Hot Zone.* We figured if the microbial menace killed more than a thousand people in Africa, then why couldn't it make its way to Albany or Annapolis?

With its graphic tales of people's insides liquefying, the book was more terrifying than anything Stephen King cranked out. And especially freaky for a kid with a vivid imagination: One minute you were jamming along at Super Mario, the next you could be bleeding out of every orifice and staring up through an inch of Plexiglas at doctors wearing hazmat suits all because you played with a monkey that one time. Stupid monkeys. As if we needed another reason to hate Marcel from *Friends.*

STATUS: The Ebola virus still exists, but it's been supplanted over the years as the threat-of-the-month with other diseases like Swine Flu, Bird Flu, and SARS.

FUN FACT: The 1995 movie *Outbreak* told the tale of a monkey-spread fictional Ebola-like virus. When the disease makes it to the United States, the government reacts in a typically calm and reasoned manner—by almost bombing a small California town back to the Stone Age.

Facial Hair

In 1990, Brandon and Dylan from *90210* sparked a sideburn resurgence, and sure, we could handle their too-cool-for-school cheek accessories. But soon misguided real-life males decided that if a little bit of facial ornamentation was good, more would be better. They figured wrong, and so began the Decade of Unfortunate Facial Hair, with whiskers sprouting from every facial pore. Colonel Sanders goatees. Alt-rock soul patches. Color Me Badd-ish geometric mini-beards. Razor blades wept at the prospect.

Some guys tried to emulate boy-banders A. J. McLean from Backstreet Boys and Chris Kirkpatrick from 'N Sync by donning a pencil-thin beard, but could only sprout puffy, patchy fluff. They ended up looking more like fuzzy-faced pro-wrestling manager Captain Lou Albano. Others relied on facial hair to define a chin where there was no chin before.

Brandon and Dylan eventually shaved, but the terrible trend they spawned continues to sprout stubbly, scraggly hair disasters on faces from coast to coast, leaving a generation looking like they're either on vacation, unemployed, or Kevin Federline.

STATUS: Like it or not, freakish facial hair is back in vogue, and comes in both traditional and ironic flavors. Brad Pitt and Joaquin Phoenix should both get permanent places in the Facial Hair Hall of Shame for their bushy, Rip Van Winkle beards.

FUN FACT: In an informal 2006 poll about facial hair in *New York* magazine, goatees received a "zero-percent approval rating." We're surprised it wasn't lower.

Fanny Packs

"**Hey,** anybody happen to have a ham sandwich?" "Why, yes, I've got one right here in my fanny pack, next to a half-eaten roll of Sucrets and an old comb." Gross, yes. But, oh so convenient! The perfect companion to Bermuda shorts and black socks, fanny packs quickly became synonymous with out-of-place tourists around the world. Worn under the belly, they were like an out-of-fashion belt that swallowed an even more out-of-fashion suitcase.

Originally—and legitimately—used by bikers, skiers, and big-city denizens who wanted to keep their valuables away from pick-pockets' grabby fingers, the convenient pouches soon were co-opted by people who simply thought carrying things was too much work. Millions of people did their best impersonation of slightly nerdy kangaroos, and suddenly fanny packs became the must-have

accessory. The upside: With the flick of a zipper, you had your wallet, passport, or sub sandwich within easy reach. The downside: They added six inches to many folks' already considerable waistlines.

STATUS: They're back, and now they're called "hands-free bags," and—believe it or not—are part of fashion haute couture. One handbag designer has a version made out of alligator for sale for two thousand dollars.

FUN FACT: Designer Isaac Mizrahi has called fanny packs one of the most reviled accessories in modern culture.

Fargo

Aw, geez." In *Fargo*, the Coen Brothers' 1996 gem, the Minnesooohta accents were as thick as ice on Leech Lake. The dark-as-a-winter-night movie introduced the world to a specially creepy corner of the upper Midwest, not to mention pregnant small-town sheriff Marge Gunderson as she headed from Brainerd, Minnesota, to the big city of Minneapolis to solve a triple homicide.

Fargo is filled with tiny moments that stick with you like a tongue to a frozen flagpole. The scene where William H. Macy's Jerry Lundegaard frantically scrapes at his ice-covered windshield as he realizes his plan is falling apart. Marge interviewing two Minnesota-Nice hookers ("Go, Bears"). The delightfully random scene where Marge has a drink with pathetic high-school classmate

Mike Yanagita ("You were such a super lady"). And we'll never look at a wood chipper the same way again. Poor Steve Buscemi.

Is *Fargo* one of the finest flicks about the ice-covered, complicated, and quirky Midwest? You betcha.

STATUS: In 2012, FX announced that it was developing a TV series of the movie—sixteen years after it came out.

FUN FACT: Not a single frame of the movie was actually shot in Fargo.

Father of the Bride

From the first moment Steve Martin stared lovingly at his daughter and her gigantic eyebrows, it was clear as a diamond engagement ring that the 1991 flick *Father of the Bride* was a mush-fest of epic proportions. Thankfully for the sarcastic kids in the audience, though, the sentiment factor was tempered by Martin's trademark shtick. Who else but the Artist Formerly Known as the Guy with the Arrow Through His Head could pull off a scene where he dangled outside a window while his soon-to-be in-laws chatted away unaware inside?

The plot was simple: Martin, as beleaguered suburban dad George Banks, fretted about his daughter's (fuzzy-browed Kimberly Williams) impending wedding, while Diane Keaton and Kieran Culkin tried to keep him from having a nervous breakdown. But the real star of the show was Martin Short as Franck, a diva-esque wedding planner with a marble-mouthed accent who chased after swans and goofed up the valet parking. His best bit was mispronouncing "cake" so it sounded more like something that you'd find in an erotic bakery.

The thing is: Now that some of us who watched this 1991 flick with our eyes rolled back in our "What. Ever" heads have daughters of our own, we get it: Growing older can be a mixed bag. Damn, Steve Martin—you taught us a valuable lesson, wrapped in something borrowed, something blue, and a whole lot of slapstick.

STATUS: The flick spawned a sequel, with Martin's character struggling with becoming a grandfather and late-in-life dad at the same time.

FUN FACT: George Banks is also the name of the dad from *Mary Poppins*.

Fax Machines

Eeee-ooooh! Before email, before text, the only real way to communicate quickly with people you didn't want to actually talk with was to send a fax. At first the ultra-high-tech method of communication was embraced only by office jokers, who sent pictures of their butts flying across phone lines. But soon everybody with a document they needed to send bypassed the post office and instead jammed their boring quarterly report into a gigantic, mechanical beast that ate rolls of paper and gulped down toner.

It was hardly foolproof. People regularly tried to fax something to a regular phone, and whoever picked up got an earful of screeches and screams. "Hello? Hmm ... sounds like the Tallahassee office is trying to send us that contract. I can't quite hear the final paragraph, though. Also, are my ears supposed to be bleeding like this?"

When it did actually connect, the sending machine inevitably jammed, so all that spit out at the other end was a smeary Rorschach test. And good luck faxing a photo, which came across as a big box of black. ("Here's the shot I took during the eclipse.")

STATUS: Many offices still have the antiquated clunkers but the technology is quickly losing ground to scanning and email.

FUN FACT: A joke version of Martha Stewart's Christmas Calendar has the domestic diva faxing her family Christmas letter to the Pulitzer committee for consideration.

Floppy Disks

If information is power, then the dawn of the 3.5-inch floppy disk made us into gods. Suck it, pencil and paper! We could now fit a whopping 1.44 megabytes in our pockets. Okay, it seemed like a lot at the time, but today it's the size of a single, blurry photo.

And with great technology came great annoyance. Sometimes we'd pop the disks into the computer and they'd make a horrific *kak-kak-kak* sound, like a cat choking on a digital hairball. Or they'd get stuck in the drive and we'd desperately unwind a paper clip, poke it in the emergency-eject hole and hold our breath that our biology paper hadn't been wiped clean. And we'd inevitably knock over a huge stack of the brightly colored plastic squares before we had a chance to label them, spewing uncontrolled rainbow chaos all over the floor.

For a while in the '90s, computer games came on both 3.5-inch and the larger—but on-the-way-out—5.25-inch floppies. People would inevitably buy the wrong one, folding and cramming the thing into a too-small drive because they simply had to play *Trump Castle 3* or *Freddy Pharkas: Frontier Pharmacist* right this second.

Hope sprung eternal with the arrival of the Iomega Zip drive in 1994. We could fit a whole computer's worth of backup on the things. Too bad the drives we needed to use them set us back two hundred dollars a piece, and were quickly rendered obsolete.

STATUS: CDs, DVDs, and flash drives all signed the floppy's death certificate. Which was probably too big to fit on a disk.

FUN FACT: Even a 16GB flash drive, which is on the small side, holds more than eleven thousand times as much information as the average floppy.

Forrest Gump

We'd already chuckled at Tom Hanks in flicks like *Big*, *Sleepless in Seattle*, and *Turner & Hooch*. (Okay, maybe not so much *Turner & Hooch*.) But with his southern-fried performance in the 1994 Oscar-winner *Forrest Gump*, Hanks shot to a new level of superstardom, wiping out every last memory of when he wore a bra and girdle in *Bosom Buddies*, or played Elyse Keaton's ne'er-do-well brother on *Family Ties*.

In the movie—a perfect blend of blow-your-nose-in-your-popcorn tear-jerker and punch-in-the-gut comedy—simpleton Forrest insinuated himself into just about every grainy piece of archival footage director Robert Zemeckis could unearth. Forrest, it seems, changed the course of history: He taught Elvis how to swivel his hips, started the ping-pong craze, exposed the Watergate break-in, and showed president Lyndon Johnson that he was shot "in the butt-tocks." He left catchphrase after catchphrase in his wake, as he pined for his childhood sweetheart Jenn-ay ("Run, Forrest! Run!"), befriended slack-jawed Bubba ("Shrimp soup, shrimp stew, shrimp salad . . ."), and sprinted across the country ("Stupid is as stupid does").

And we watched it all over and over again, until we could recite every line by heart. Every time we popped it into the VCR, unlike the box of chocolates Forrest carried around, we knew exactly what we were gonna get.

STATUS: The book *Forrest Gump* has a sequel, *Gump and Co.*, and there's constant talk of making a movie sequel out of it, but nothing yet.

FUN FACT: According to IMDb.com, John Travolta, Chevy Chase, and Bill Murray all turned down the role that eventually went to Hanks.

FoxTrot

What *Peanuts* was to the 1950s, Bill Amend's *FoxTrot* was to the 1990s. But while Charlie Brown and pals were oblivious to the pop culture of their era, dorky dad Roger and mom Andy's three kids bathe in it. Oldest son Peter adores Bruce Springsteen and Cindy Crawford, boy-crazy sister Paige decks her room with *90210* posters, and youngest kid Jason writes computer viruses and is obsessed with *Star Wars*.

Amend majored in physics, and it shows, especially in his

dead-on portrayal of brainy, geeky Jason. When Jason and pal Marcus plan a snow fort, it has twelve missile silos. After they see *Jurassic Park*, Jason writes a letter to PBS telling them Barney should be eating the kids. His diorama on the Great Depression features Kirk, Spock, and Bones jumping back through a time portal.

But you don't have to know Klingon to feel like the Foxes are part of your family. Jason may play Nintendo instead of baseball and own an iguana instead of a beagle, but like *Peanuts*, *FoxTrot* has a universality and a heart that defies time periods. And Jason's moved from loving *Star Trek* to *Star Wars* to *Avatar*, from iMacs to iPads, without batting an eye—or aging beyond age ten. The geek shall inherit the earth.

STATUS: *FoxTrot* ended as a daily comic strip in 2006, moving to Sundays only.

FUN FACT: In one episode of *The Sopranos*, mob boss Tony and son A.J. are seen reading *FoxTrot* in their Sunday paper. Maybe Jason makes them an offer they can't refuse.

Free Willy

When the title of your movie makes an entire theater full of preteen boys collapse in a fit of giggles and snort Orange Crush out of their noses, you probably want to fire whatever focus group told you it was a good idea. 1993's *Free Willy* had one of the worst titles in cinematic history. They couldn't have come up with a different name for the whale? How about Steve? Steve is a good, middle-of-the-road whale name. And, most important, doesn't make people think of a wang.

Terrible title aside, the movie, about a twelve-year-old boy befriending a five-ton killer whale, had us all bawling out of our blowholes. The '90s were a good time to be a cute kid who could turn on the waterworks because of an animal friend, like Anna Paquin and her geese in *Fly Away Home* or Tina Majorino and her Hawaiian-shirt-wearing seal BFF, Andre. Jason James Richter, the kid from *Free Willy*, didn't exactly parlay his success as a child actor into a sustained career, though. Your acting gigs tend to dry up when you're best known for playing second fiddle to a giant pile of blubber.

STATUS: They freed Willy in three sequels and a cartoon. And people still love whale tales. In 2012's *Big Miracle*, Drew Barrymore and John Krasinski tried to save a family of gray whales stuck in the ice.

FUN FACT: In the 1994 animated series on ABC, Willy and his boy Jesse teamed up to fight the Machine, a cyborg out to pollute the oceans.

Friends

Our friends looked nothing like this. Forget Manhattan, even in Minneapolis no one had an apartment as spacious as Monica's. Or a hairstyle as trendsetting as Rachel's, sarcasm as sharp as Chandler's, or the sexy airheadedness of Joey. These were fictional "friends" for sure, but spending time with them was often hilarious and always entertaining.

Gorgeous they may have been, but like most twentysomethings in the 1990s, the "friends" were embarrassingly underemployed. How else could they spend so much time hanging at Central Perk, singing about a certain "Smelly Cat," or watching embarrassing prom videos from the 1980s? Love was hard to come by too. The Ross-Rachel, yes-no, love-hate relationship wore thin, but just when it vaulted into cliché, the writers managed to save it. (*"We were on a break!"*)

But what really endeared fans to these "friends" were the little things. The trivia contest where no one knew what Chandler's job was, Ross bleaching his teeth so much they glowed in the dark, the Thanksgiving football game where Ross and Monica refought childhood battles. Through it all, though, ran a ribbon of devotion. The *Seinfeld* crew was one chocolate babka away from every man for himself, but the "friends" were truly there for each other, just as their theme song claimed.

STATUS: Gone for good—except in reruns or on DVDs. *How I Met Your Mother* may be for the Nintendo generation what *Friends* was for the Atari era.

Fruit by the Foot

In the 1990s, Fruit Roll-Ups took a lesson from major-league baseball and started injecting themselves with growth hormones. They then gave birth to Fruit by the Foot, a yard-long version of the original 1980s snacking favorite.

The three-foot length made it as much of a toy as a treat. Who didn't paste a couple rolls together and use it to measure your height, or your dog's? Between this and the enormous roll of gum

that was Bubble Tape, what was the message being sent to 1990s kids here? Snarf down twice as much junk food as your Gen X siblings ever did just to keep up? Was it all some giant corporate test of a new generation's self-control? If so, we failed. Deliciously.

Hippie moms bought food dehydrators and made their own, which went over about as well as when they tried substituting carob for chocolate. We universally preferred the packaged stuff, although to be honest, they contained about as much "fruit" as they did "foot."

STATUS: Still for sale, including tie-dye and mystery flavors.

FUN FACT: In a creepy 1990s commercial, the smiley face on a kid's T-shirt eats up his Fruit by the Foot. TV addicts spent much too much time pondering the physics of how that was even possible.

Furby

It was part Giga Pet, part Gizmo from *Gremlins*: Furby was the Cabbage Patch Kid of 1998, as desperate parents knocked each other down at the Toys R Us to bring home the hairy, animatronic alien for their mesmerized child.

Out of the box, the battery-operated fuzz ball spoke only "Furbish," nonsensical gibberish. But kids could "teach" him English—the more you played with him, the more he made sense. You could interact with him by petting his back or sticking your finger in his mouth. Sure, we all knew the Furby was using every ounce of his alien willpower not to chomp through our flesh and suckle human blood, but they were so cute, we didn't care.

Just like real parents, Furby moms and dads eventually knew sweet joy when their little guy uttered those three little words every kid longed to hear from a pet: "I love you." Sure, now they're mostly screaming for help getting out of the box in the attic you threw them in, but hey, nobody said love was forever.

STATUS: In 2012, Furby 2.0 hit stores from Hasbro, now with backlit LCD eyes, an available iPad app, and a price that's about twice as much as it was in the 1990s.

FUN FACT: The little guy's resemblance to Gizmo the Mogwai from the hit 1984 movie *Gremlins* didn't go unnoticed: According to *Variety*, Hasbro settled with Warner Bros. for a reported seven-figure payout.

Gak

Gak was thicker and less gelatinous than its boogery ancestor, '70s gross-out staple Slime, but it was no less entertaining. Especially when you squeezed it and it made farty noises. A cross between Silly Putty, Play-Doh, and snot, Gak came in an amoeba-shaped container and smelled like ammonia and rotten milk. Still—or maybe because of that—it was the most popular in Mattel's Nickelodeon line of products named after choking sounds. (Others: Smud, Goooze, and Floam.)

Gak's label featured several bold-printed cautions, the most intriguing of which was: "Gak is not a food product." Were kids spreading this stuff on toast? Or snapping off a hunk and chewing it like gum? Whether or not they ingested it, nobody heeded the other warning: "Caution: Do not play with Gak on carpeting." Run your hands through the wall-to-wall in any '90s house, and you'll find twenty-year-old Gak still clinging to every fiber. The stuff's persistent, we'll give it that.

In the mid-90s, Mattel embraced Gak's inner stinkitude, and launched a line with added scents called Smell My Gak. Pickles, pizza, or hot dogs, anyone? Uh, one word, and it's not the name of a Mattel product: Blorf.

STATUS: Gak came back in 2012.

FUN FACT: You could also get a Gak Vac, a handheld pump that let you suck up the Gak and then squirt it out—most likely onto the carpet.

Game Boy

Our older siblings had Mattel Electronic Football, but in 1989, we got something far more revolutionary: Nintendo's Game Boy and its monochromatic, 8-bit freedom of choice. Unlike earlier handheld consoles, you could actually change the game you were playing. *Tetris* one minute, *Alleyway* the next. It put portable, versatile gaming power in our twelve-year-old hands, and most important, gifted us with the ability to feed our short attention spans by yanking one cartridge and replacing it with another. Buh-bye, *Super Mario*—see you again when my Ritalin wears off.

Very few of us minded that the screen was the size of a piece of Dentyne. Yes, we had to squint like pirates to make out what the microscopic guys in *Bill & Ted's Excellent Game Boy Adventure* were up to. (Answer: We're still not sure.) Until Game Boy Color hit stores in 1998, that is. The screen wasn't any bigger, but the color was a revelation, like when Dorothy opened up the door of her tornado-swept house and inhaled a Technicolor Munchkinland. Our eyes were glued to the colorful but still tiny screen; we weren't looking up for anything. The system should have prompted a new slogan: Game Boy—Prepping a generation for texting and walking since 1989.

STATUS: In 2004, Nintendo unveiled the DS, which meant game over for Game Boy.

FUN FACT: Nintendo released the Game Boy Camera in 1998, which took super-grainy black-and-white photos, and for a time was recognized by Guinness as the smallest digital camera in the world.

George Foreman Grill

Kids of the '90s were too young to remember George Foreman for his famed Rumble in the Jungle with Muhammad Ali in 1974. Instead they knew the boxer as a genial bald man who had a ton of kids named after him and who made delicious-looking burgers.

Has there ever been a more extreme personality change in American history? Foreman as a fighter was a stone-cold badass, with muscles of steel and a grim murderous look. Foreman as a commercial pitchman was a cartoon of a man with a permanent smile, dorky apron, and ability to say things like "Knocks out the fat!" and "With built-in bun warmer!" without cracking up.

Sure, you could keep on making burgers on the stove or outside on the grill, but America loves nothing more than a new gadget, especially one endorsed by a celebrity. In an era when everyone had closets stuffed full of seldom-used appliances, the Foreman Grill punched its way into our kitchens and rope-a-doped the other items fighting for counter space. Down goes the juicer! Down goes the bread machine!

STATUS: Still cooking, in many sizes and colors.

FUN FACT: Wrestler Hulk Hogan reportedly was going to be asked to endorse the grill, but he wasn't home, so Foreman got the call—and the millions.

Giant Cell Phones

The first time a lot of us laid eyes on a "cellular telephone" was in 1989, when early adopter Zack Morris beeped and booped his way into TV history on *Saved by the Bell*. It looked like a high-tech loaf of bread, smelled like something burning, and thanks to its heft, probably gave Mark-Paul Gosselaar years of back trouble. But it did allow him to get into all sorts of hijinks, including ordering pizza in class and calling Screech while pretending to be a girl.

Cell phones slowly started to move into our world too, and man, at first we felt like *Wall Street* king Gordon Gekko. If you were lucky enough to get one of the first cell phones—perhaps due to a paranoid mom who was willing to fork over the big bucks so she could track your every move—you know it wasn't exactly sleek. Holding one up to your ear was like bashing the side of your head with a brick. Forget shoving them in your pocket either. Girls with purses the size of an unabridged dictionary could cram them in there, but boys were pretty much outta luck.

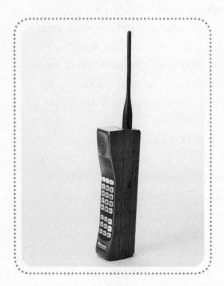

Not that you got to make many calls on them though. Parents were so paranoid about bills that they warned their kids to only use them in emergencies. No calling to remind Mom to pick you up from practice. They were for when you broke your leg—but only if the bone was visible. For a sprain, you could wait in line for the pay phone.

STATUS: Who still has a landline? Mobile phones are everywhere. With the introduction of the Razr in 2004, they shrunk so significantly, they were almost choking hazards.

FUN FACT: There's a whole website devoted to Zack's humongous phone: ZackMorrisCellPhone.com.

Goosebumps Books

Mom might have been toting her Stephen King paperback, but kids of the 1990s could match her fright for fright with a scary book of their own from R. L. Stine's Goosebumps series. Forget the musty old campfire tales of ghosts and one-eyed pirates. These tales took terror into a modern kid's world, whether they were stuck inside a haunted Halloween mask or trapped in a sarcophagus inside an Egyptian pyramid.

Sure, Stine's characters found themselves in situations we'd only seen in nightmares, but they felt real because he sketched them out as normal kids, fighting with siblings and worrying about being popular. Oh, and dealing with giant worms, cursed cameras, and cuckoo clocks that can send you back in time.

And as with anything kids loved this much, inevitably, there was a backlash. As scary as the books could be, they were never violent or cruel. Yet that didn't stop the imagination police from

trying to ban them from school libraries, either for being too scary or for containing suggestions of the occult. Yeah, show us a kid who was led to Satanism because of a goofy Goosebumps story and we'll show you a kid who decided to play in traffic because it looked like so much fun in *Frogger*.

STATUS: Stine still writes six Goosebumps books a year. A new Goosebumps series, Hall of Horrors, launched in 2011. The first book, *Claws*, is about a zombie cat.

FUN FACT: A 1995 parody series, Gooflumps, offered up two titles, *Eat Cheese and Barf* (playing off of *Say Cheese and Die*) and *Stay Out of the Bathroom* (a twist on *Stay Out of the Basement*).

Got Milk? Ad Campaign

The very first "Got Milk?" ad, which aired in 1993, remains the best. A radio station will give a guy ten thousand dollars if he can tell them who shot Alexander Hamilton, and his entire apartment is a museum to that famous duel. Yet with a mouth full of peanut butter and no milk, he can't spit out the answer. "Aaron Burr" comes out vaguely sounding like *"Aawhahn Buhhe!"*

Later ads turned amazingly edgy and dark for a dairy-product campaign. Cats menace a sweet elderly lady who tries to fool them with nondairy creamer. A Damien-like boy warns others not to eat the cake at the world's creepiest birthday party. Full Body Cast Man snarfs down a cookie but can't make his beverage request understood.

"Got Milk?" spawned an entire industry of unfunny parodies, from "Got beer?" to "Got MILF?" But nothing touches the original. Milk is always missing, people are always tortured for the want of it. In the world of empty milk cartons, the lactose intolerant is king.

STATUS: The catchphrase is still popular.

FUN FACT: That very first "Got Milk?" ad was directed by Hollywood explosion master Michael Bay, who would go on to direct the *Transformers* films. Got dynamite?

Groundhog Day

Plenty of '90s movies were perfect for watching and rewatching until our VCRs spat out the tape in disgust—but only one did the rewinding for us: *Groundhog Day*. When his alarm clock flicked over from 5:59 to 6:00, Bill Murray rolled out of bed to the strains of Sonny and Cher's "I Got You, Babe" and quickly realized that he was trapped in the same day over and over again. He'd interact with the goofy denizens of Punxsutawney, Pennsylvania ("Bing!"), hit the hay, and when he woke up the next morning, it all started over again.

Once he realized nothing he did had consequences, a snarky and bored Murray embraced his inner hedonist, stuffing a whole piece of cake into his mouth while sucking down a cigarette, and using his repeating reality to charm a hot townie into the sack. Eventually, Murray started to warm to the townspeople, realized he was being a jerk, and used his superpowers to help them rather than take advantage. Bing! The curse broke—along with Murray's crunchy outer shell.

Critics praised the flick for its spiritual take on the nature of existence. We loved it because Murray kept his trademark smarm even as he became a better person. The film couldn't have been cast better. After starring in 2006's horrible *Garfield: A Tail of Two Kitties*, doesn't Murray of all people deserve a do-over?

STATUS: Especially around February 2, it keeps coming back on TV . . . again and again.

FUN FACT: According to IMDb.com, Murray was bitten twice by the groundhog in the film.

Grunge

The poppy, bright sounds of '80s music gave way in the '90s to the blunt, honest notes of grunge, pouring like rain off the damp streets of Seattle. The music was pulled together the same way the musicians assembled their flannel-heavy, thrift-store wardrobes, with disparate elements of punk, metal, and alternative music all forming an uneasy alliance. It seemed to spring straight from the hearts of the ignored kids who slouched in the back of the gym during school assemblies, who never showed up for football games and proms.

The lyrics, when you could understand them, freaked parents out. Rest assured, the Beach Boys never led off a song with "load up on guns, and bring your friends," and Duran Duran probably never felt "stupid and contagious."

The genre had style, sure, but it was a complete rejection of what had passed for rock chic in previous eras. Hairspray and carefully feathered locks felt fake and showy next to built-for-comfort flannels and white-boy dreads. Who needed to bathe in a tub when you could bathe daily in your own angst and ennui?

Nirvana's Kurt Cobain, who would become the marquee name of the genre, represented every kid who never fit in, whether due to a broken home, crappy school experience, or just a messed-up self-image. Cobain himself once expressed shock that the fans he saw wearing Nirvana T-shirts were the same kind of kids who'd once beaten him up.

Grunge soared high and burned out fast, with Cobain's 1994 suicide marking an end point for many. But it was in its time the perfect soundtrack for a generation raised with low expectations, coming too late to a party that was making them no promises.

STATUS: Many say punkier, poppier young bands like Green Day and Blink-182 were grunge's most natural successors.

FUN FACT: Teen Spirit deodorant, the brand which inadvertently inspired the name of Nirvana's hit, soared in the 1990s thanks to the song's popularity, but then started to fade. Now only two of its ten scents remain.

Hacky Sack

E ven kids who grew up in the uber-organized sports leagues of the 1980s eventually mellowed out enough to embrace the unofficial sport of the '90s, Hacky Sack. Oddly enough for a nation that has long hated soccer, American teens welcomed this sport with open feet, despite the fact that it's really just soccer with a smaller ball and less of that sweat-inducing running.

Almost every guy who was in his teens in the 1990s, from football captain to D&D nerd, can look back on at least a few sunny

hours joyously wasted kicking a little beanbag around their high school field or college quad.

Speaking of "wasted," is there a Hacky Sack anywhere on the planet that does not reek of pot smoke? If there is, it almost certainly smells of spilled Mountain Dew Slurpee and barbecue potato chips. Hacky Sack embraced its stoner vibe proudly. If there was a game you could imagine Shaggy from *Scooby-Doo* playing, this is it.

STATUS: Still getting kicked around.

FUN FACT: Hacky Sack is a trademarked brand, but the game played with it is actually called "footbag."

Happy Fun Ball

I t's just a minute and a half long, but the "Happy Fun Ball" commercial parody that aired on *Saturday Night Live* in 1991 is a classic that can sit right up there next to Dan Aykroyd's Bass-o-matic or Bad Idea Jeans.

You remember: The innocuous looking red ball comes with an unending list of warnings, delivered in the soothingly dulcet tones of Phil Hartman. "Happy Fun Ball may stick to certain types of skin." Its liquid core should not be "touched, inhaled, or looked at." And then, the big revelation: Happy Fun Ball's ingredients "include an unknown glowing substance which fell to Earth, presumably from outer space," and it "is being dropped from our warplanes on Iraq." And the line everyone remembers, quotes, and repurposes: "Do not taunt Happy Fun Ball." If this didn't lead you to envision the carnage that would ensue if you disobeyed, you, my friend, have not read nearly enough Stephen King novels.

Happy Fun Ball was simple and ingenious. Even though the skit's two decades old, it's worked its way so deep into our pop-culture fabric that no amount of taunting will remove it. Not that we plan to try. We might have that certain type of skin.

STATUS: You can check it out on *SNL* skit collections and on YouTube.

FUN FACT: The sketch was written by Jack Handey, of "Deep Thoughts" fame.

Have You Ever...
You Will!

This series of futuristic AT&T TV commercials were a mix of completely whacked and utterly prescient. Featuring the soothing narration of Tom Selleck, each ad demonstrated three not-that-far-off scenarios and bragged that they would soon be delivered by the communications company.

Some were nuts. "Have you ever sent a fax from the beach?" Good Lord, who wants to? This segment also had no idea that faxing was about to become as outdated as smoke signals.

But others were scarily right on. "Have you ever had an assistant who lived in your computer?" Hello, iPhone's Siri. "Have you ever crossed the country without stopping to ask directions?" Thank you, in-car GPS. "Have you ever watched the movie you wanted to, when you wanted to?" Video on demand or Netflix streaming, anyone?

Sure, not all of the eventual breakthroughs came from AT&T, but still, watching these ads was a little like sitting in 1993 and getting passed notes from Future You in 2013. It was a damn shame you couldn't send along lottery numbers or stock picks while you were at it. Get on that, Future You.

STATUS: AT&T continued trying to position itself as the company with its finger on the pulse of tomorrow by using ads that urged customers to "Rethink Possible."

Home Alone

Yes, back in the 1990s, the tale of an eight-year-old boy left alone in his house while criminals tried to break in was considered hilarious fodder for movies. In real life, the story would have led the nightly news, and ended with a Macaulay Culkin–shaped chalk outline on the floor.

But in 1990's *Home Alone*, it was a hoot. Yes, we suspended disbelief as little fishy-lipped Kevin McAllister took on robbers Joe Pesci and Daniel Stern using nothing more than his ingenuity and a few items he found around the house, MacGyver-style. Where did Kevin get his elaborate booby-trap training—the CIA? He also showed pretty severe psychotic tendencies and more than a little bloodlust. Pesci and Stern were trying to break into the house, but Culkin was trying to *kill* them, with a blowtorch to the head, a hot iron to the face, a BB gun to the pants, and Micro Machines beneath their feet.

We kids luckily never had to deal with a robber taking us on mano a mano in our own house, but after this movie, man, we dreamed about it. If only Mom and Dad would forget about us long enough for us to set up an uber-complicated network of traps of our own. That Avon lady, cookie-peddling Girl Scout, or pesky guy selling aluminum siding would never know what hit 'em.

STATUS: The original movie sparked a 1992 sequel, with Kevin on his own in New York, and a third flick, where Macaulay Culkin was replaced by bowl-haircut-headed Alex D. Linz, plus a 2002 TV movie.

FUN FACT: The suburban Chicago house featured in the movie sold in 2012 for $1.5 million, paint cans in the face not included.

Hypercolor

Hypercolor heat-sensitive clothing made people into real-life mood rings. Don a purple Hypercolor shirt and have your friend slap you on the back . . . voila, pink handprint.

It sounded cool when you bought the shirt, but Hypercolor was a pretty weird technology. Hey, nice pink spots in your sweaty armpits, dude! Is that a pair of Hypercolor pants or are you just happy to see me? Nerds would sport a Hypercolor shirt in the hope that the cute girl in math would be unable to keep her hands off them, but let us be frank, that never happened. Instead it was your own friends and the occasional hallway dork who smacked you or, worse, rubbed their snotty nose on you to make the color change.

Sadly or thankfully, once you washed the shirt enough, it

would no longer do its little trick, and you could resume sweating with impunity.

STATUS: Chains like American Apparel rediscovered Hypercolor around 2008.

FUN FACT: Hypercolor's opposite was a brand of winter gloves called Freezy Freakies, which displayed patterns when it got cold enough.

If You Give a Mouse a Cookie Books

First, in 1985, there was Laura Numeroff's popular picture book, *If You Give a Mouse a Cookie*. But then the food-items-to-animal giving took off in a big way, and soon pigs were getting pancakes, cats devouring cupcakes, moose receiving muffins, and the original cookie-taking mouse was going to school, the movies, and heaven knows where else. Hopefully a bakery, where he could buy his own damn cookie.

This book format was quickly memorized by every kid, parent, and babysitter in the 1990s and beyond. Once the animal received their treat, they started to get demanding. The mouse wanted milk to go with his cookie; the cat, sprinkles to accompany her cupcake; the pig, syrup for its pancake. And if you think it's a good idea to give such potentially mess-producing items to small mammals, think again. Milk will result in demands for straws, sprinkle requests will somehow turn into beach visits, syrup will lead to baths. Where will the greed end?

Yet the narrators of these books never learned. They continued the unrestrained giving! This only led to disaster, with pigs seeking out tap shoes, and eventually building elaborate tree houses that for whatever reason required eight metric tons of wallpaper. We're still not sure how working out at the gym inspired the cat to want to go to the park and then the science museum, but ours is not to reason why.

This much we know: If you read a kid a *Give a Thing a Thing* book, pretty soon she's going to ask you for another one. And if you read her another one—well, you get the picture.

STATUS: Still extremely popular.

FUN FACT: Numeroff's autobiography is called *If You Give an Author a Pencil.*

"I'm Gonna Be (500 Miles)"

T he Doublemint Twins were annoyingly perky. The creepy identical ghost girls in *The Shining* freaked us out. But in the 1990s, the set o' lookalike siblings that most people wanted deported were the pasty, bespectacled Scottish brothers Charlie and Craig Reid, better known as The Proclaimers. Their crime?

Unleashing the earworm to end all earworms on an unsuspecting nation with the 1993 hit, "I'm Gonna Be (500 Miles)."

You know the song—and your therapist probably does too. "Buht *Ayyyye* wouhld walk fah-ve hundred miles ahnd *Ayyyye* wouhld walk fah-ve hun-dred moooooore . . ." Romantic, sure, but actually, that's a terrible idea, sure to give you hospitalization-level blisters and a scorching sunburn.

The twins may have sung it, but we have Johnny Depp to blame for its 1990s ubiquity. The bouncy tune hit the charts—and burrowed its way into our brains—as part of the soundtrack to the Depp film *Benny & Joon*. The song was kind of like haggis: It must have seemed like a good idea originally, but about thirty seconds in, you wanted to squeeze the singers' heads like bagpipes.

STATUS: Still popping up on certain radio stations. All it takes is a couple seconds of the catchy, nonsensical chorus and you're humming it for weeks. "Da da dun da. Da da dun da. Undela undela undela la la la." You're welcome.

FUN FACT: A running joke on the CBS show *How I Met Your Mother* revolves around a tape of the song that's permanently stuck in Marshall's car stereo.

"I'm the King of the World!"

Remember when it was supercool to stand on the front of a boat, spread your arms wide, and yell, "I'm the king of the world!" like Leonardo DiCaprio famously did in 1997's *Titanic*? Yeah, it never was. But supercool or not, everybody who had seen the movie struck the pose, no matter if they were on a luxury liner or in a canoe.

It was as if we were compelled: Water + boat = an uncontrollable urge to inappropriately call attention to ourselves by screaming lame dialogue from a movie. (In 2004, it was voted the cheesiest movie line ever, even beating out "Nobody puts Baby in a corner" from *Dirty Dancing*.)

Little known fact: There's actually no such thing as the king of the world. The reality is that Earth is made up of many countries, each of which has its own leader. One person doesn't actually govern the entire thing. Although with the wind in his face and a sweet job like coal shoveler in the bowels of a ship on his résumé, it's no wonder DiCaprio's character truly felt like he had the world at his feet. Too bad he also had an iceberg looming in his peripheral vision.

STATUS: People are apparently still using this phrase in conversation. In 2011, police in Florida Tased a man three times after he ran naked into traffic, screaming the memorable line.

FUN FACT: *Titanic* director James Cameron delivered the line when he took home the Oscar for Best Director. He was not Tased, although perhaps he should have been.

Inline Skates

We couldn't roller skate, we couldn't ice skate, and suddenly in the 1990s, we couldn't do both at the same time. Inline skates like Rollerblades combined the wheels of roller skates with the one-single-blade design of ice skates, supposedly to let hockey players stay in shape in warm weather months. Most people, however, wore them to flirt with cute strangers around city lakes and parks, ticking off bicyclists and occasionally going head over wheels straight into some oblivious mom pushing a stroller.

Inline skates worked pretty well if you were capable of getting them moving, but heaven help you if you ever wanted to come to a complete stop. There was a chunky brake included, but that worked about as smoothly as Fred Flintstone putting his feet down to stop his prehistoric car. Everyone we knew was able to stop only by stumbling headfirst onto a patch of grass, or worse, straight into a tree.

Fortunately, whoever sold you the blades probably also upsold you on some knee, wrist, and elbow pads, plus a helmet. Unfortunately, they were probably still sitting in the box in your closet, since it was much cooler to risk a concussion than to look like a bubble-wrapped dork.

STATUS: Still rolling.

FUN FACT: There's a 1991 martial arts movie, *The Roller Blade Seven*, about a post-apocalyptic world where people travel only on skates and skateboards. Of course Frank Stallone is in it.

"I've Fallen and I Can't Get Up" Ads

You remember. Old Mrs. Fletcher wipes out in her bathroom, hollers the now-infamous line, and presumably is saved by medic-alert service LifeCall before she's eaten alive by her (certainly thousands of) cats. From the Dolly Parton–esque hair of the concerned daughter to the whiny diction of the star ("Oi've *Fawwen!*"), the spot offered more cheese than a deli.

The phrase became the 1990s version of "Where's the beef?" There were musical remixes, endless parodies, a mention in a Weird Al song, a *Roseanne* reference, and mocking shirts ("I've Fallen and I Can't Reach My Beer").

Sure, old people taking dives isn't funny, but damn, this ad was.

STATUS: LifeCall went out of business in 1993, but similar company Life Alert trademarked the slogan and still uses it. Other catchphrase-causing ads since then have included "Head

On! Apply it to your forehead" and Subway's ubiquitous "Five! Five-dollar! Five-dollar footlong!"

FUN FACT: In one MadTV parody, a dense elderly couple think their medical-alert button is the remote control. Their attempt at channel changing calls the paramedics, which freaks the oldsters out so much they dash outside and are run over by a semi.

Janet Reno's Dance Party

Quick, who's the U.S. attorney general? In the late '90s, every kid in the country knew—thanks to Will Ferrell's impersonation of a certain A.G. with a mannish 'do, deep voice, and bright blue outfit. On *Saturday Night Live*'s recurring "Janet Reno's Dance Party" sketch, Ferrell portrayed the first female attorney general as a defensive, clench-fisted, karate-choppin' force of nature in pearls and sensible pumps—who also happened to be throwing a party for local kids in her unfinished basement. Amid the crepe paper, balloons, and disco ball, Ferrell would stop to interview students, and quickly accuse them all of lying ("Shut your mouth, you dirty liar"), or dive into the crowd ("Here comes 180 pounds of pure Reno!").

Watching "Reno" herky-jerk to "My Sharona" or slow dance with then–Secretary of Health Donna Shalala (Kevin Spacey!) blew our minds, but it was seeing her in a boxing match with the real Rudy Giuliani that pushed the skit into classic territory. Ferrell kneed Giuliani in the groin, and then, when accused of boxing dirty, crazily flailed his arms and uttered one of the best retorts ever to come out of SNL: "Then how comes my conscience is so clean?!"

Taking a cue from her fictionalized self, the real-life Janet Reno hosted a dance party as a campaign fund-raiser when she ran for the governor of Florida. She didn't win.

STATUS: Available on DVD collections, Hulu, and YouTube.

FUN FACT: The actual Reno appeared on the final "Dance Party" sketch, busting through a cinder-block wall Kool-Aid Man–style.

Jell-O Jigglers

Jell-O wasn't the first gelatin company to make their product into wiggly but firm blocks that were easy to shape with cookie cutters—Knox Blox had been around for decades. But when marketing manager Dana Gioia helped launch a promotions blitz for Jell-O Jigglers in 1990, the colorful finger food was suddenly everywhere.

In a 1991 TV ad, Jell-O spokeslegend Bill Cosby advocated making Christmas-shaped Jigglers for Santa in place of milk and cookies. Egg- and jellybean-shaped molds encouraged Jigglers as an Easter treat. Kids loved them because it was suddenly okay to eat Jell-O with your fingers. Jell-O loved them because they required four times as much Jell-O to make as a regular pan of the stuff, plus they could keep cranking out holiday-themed molds.

For some kids, Jigglers were the first step into mom and dad's kitchen. They were tasty, easy, fun to eat, and the variety of colors and shapes kept things interesting. If only all foods came in every color of the rainbow and required the use of cookie cutters.

STATUS: Still jiggling.

FUN FACT: In Carolyn Wyman's book, *Jell-O: A Biography*, it's revealed that Jell-O marketers first laughed off the term "Jigglers" because it sounded obscene. But when a quick poll of Kraft secretaries revealed that the name passed muster with them, a new product was born.

The Jerry Springer Show

Are you a pregnant prostitute? Having an affair with your cousin? In love with a phone-sex operator? Proud to be a homewrecker? Cheating on your boyfriend with his identical twin? All of the above? There's one place for you, and it's center stage at *The Jerry Springer Show*, the spawned-in-the-1990s phenomenon that all but invented tabloid TV.

Springer's show was a revelation when it launched in 1991. Sure, TV hadn't exactly been all *Masterpiece Theatre* for some time, but we didn't see this tasteless talk show coming. The swearing! The punching! The blurred boobies! Security guard Steve—

who soon became a star in his own right—diving bravely into a cartoon-like ball of flying fists and hair-pulling! Jerry's insipid "Final Thought," a weirdly discombobulating statement that was about as relevant to the hillbilly guests as toothpaste!

Springer faded from the spotlight for many reasons. Once the dialogue became completely incomprehensible thanks to the necessary bleeps, it wasn't as much fun to watch the fights. And eventually, there was just no way the show could top its latest insane topic. Really, after the transvestite who cut off his/her own legs with a power saw, even boob-flashing grandmas and self-proclaimed vampires felt tame by comparison.

STATUS: Thirty-six hundred episodes strong and still screaming.

FUN FACT: Some stations refused to carry a *Springer* episode titled "I Married a Horse."

Jim Carrey

Remember when Jim Carrey was known only as the White Guy on *In Living Color*? For a brief time in the early '90s, the lanky comic's claim to fame was off-kilter characters like Vera de Milo and Fire Marshal Bill on the Fox comedy-sketch show. But then, in 1994, three of what would become his signature flicks hit the big screen, and—ssssomebody stop him!—he became a household name. (Although in many households, the conversation went: "Isn't Jim Carrey annoying?")

In *The Mask*, Carrey's "ssssmokin'!" human cartoon character romanced Cameron Diaz (in her first role) and ate up the scenery with his giant choppers. In *Dumb & Dumber*, he teamed up with the Farrelly Brothers and fellow goofball Jeff Daniels to unleash a whole new level of sophomoric—yet undeniably hilarious—humor onto cineplexes from coast to coast. ("What is the soup du jour?" "It's the soup of the day." "Mmmm—that sounds good. I'll have that.") And as *Ace Ventura: Pet Detective*, Carrey showcased his Big Boy pompadour and talked out of his butt.

Aaaall righty, then.

STATUS: Carrey eventually made the leap to more dramatic work with films like *I Love You Phillip Morris* and *Eternal Sunshine of the Spotless Mind*.

FUN FACT: According to IMDb.com, when he was ten years old, Carrey sent his résumé to *The Carol Burnett Show*.

Jim's Journal

For Jim of comic strip *Jim's Journal*, buying a scrub brush is a pretty big day. The big-headed, mouthless Wisconsinite wanders through his comic strip like many folks do through their own lives. Hardly anything major happens in his four-panel strips. In one, he sits at Dairy Queen idly watching an ant crawl across the table. In another, he ruminates about how a sore throat gets better as the day wears on.

The strip, which ran in more than two hundred college newspapers during the 1990s, followed Jim through college, numerous menial jobs, and an out-of-nowhere marriage to chum Ruth, who's oddly desperate for him to enjoy stamp collecting.

While the strips are outwardly banal, there's sometimes a germ of wisdom or humor. When Jim gets new shoelaces, he spends the day mesmerized by their gleam. After he reads *The Sound and the Fury*, he finds TV to be a lot more stupid than usual. Like most of us, Jim's life doesn't soar into mountains of joy and sink into valleys of despair, it just keeps on keeping on, Thoreau's quiet desperation measured out in stick figures.

STATUS: In 2011, *Jim's Journal* began running on GoComics .com. The new run features a mix of classic and new Jim, including a prequel where Jim is in high school (an aptitude test tells him he'd be a good dentist).

FUN FACT: Jim's creator, Scott Dikkers, later founded *The Onion*.

Juice Boxes

Back in the day, kid beverage choices were as varied as colors for Henry Ford's cars. You could have milk, or you could have this slightly warmer glass of milk. On your birthday, maybe chocolate milk. But for some reason in the late 1980s and 1990s, the Berlin Wall of beverage isolation was torn down, and juice boxes poured into the breach.

We're not sure why Mom's defenses collapsed—maybe she was too busy fighting against Twinkies or celebrating a victory for carrot sticks. But all of a sudden, squarish juice boxes were an acceptable lunch-box and after-school beverage. For kids bored with moo juice, it was like that moment in *The Wizard of Oz* when the world suddenly turns into Technicolor. You could have apple juice! Carrot-apple blends! Hi-C Ecto-Cooler, a shockingly green drink with Slimer from *Ghostbusters* on the box! Capri Sun in bizarre silver pouches! We were overwhelmed with option paralysis, our tongues never tasting the same flavor twice. Sure, the juice was probably more sugar and chemicals than anything ever grown in a garden, but "juice box" was a lot more fun to say than corn-syrup-and-citric-acid box.

Kids in the juice box era walked around with the things all but surgically attached to their lips. Juice boxes were much cooler than the standard school-issue milk carton, and half of their coolness had nothing to do with the liquid inside, and everything to do with the attached straws. You could blow bubbles, dribble, shoot liquid at the wall or your best friend. Slurping through a juice box straw was like having your tongue replaced with a snake's.

STATUS: Kids still love 'em.

FUN FACT: The Foreigner lyric "juke box hero, got stars in his eyes" is sometimes misheard as "juice box hero, got a straw in his eye."

Kid Cuisine

Heat-and-eat food for kids has been around for decades (uh, oh . . . SpaghettiO's), but in 1990, Banquet came up with Kid Cuisine, one of the first microwavable frozen meals for children. TV dinners for tots! The initial lineup featured eight extreeeeme entrées, including pizza, chicken nuggets, and macaroni and cheese with mini-franks, plus side dishes and dessert.

Kids snarfed them down. An early commercial had a boy celebrating the fact that his mom was so busy, she couldn't cook and he got to eat a Kid Cuisine meal instead of a homemade one. And why wouldn't kids start to drool over the prospect of eating fast food at home? Especially when it came packaged with an activity book with games and stickers? And also a lot of saturated fat. Plus pudding.

Even when everyone from *Consumer Reports* to nutritionists went after the trays of fat and freezer burn for their distinct lack of nutrition, parents kept serving them up, letting their kids shovel the mostly empty calories down their gullets one high-sodium forkful at a time. Mmm . . . tasted like convenience—and a little like childhood obesity.

STATUS: Today, the revamped brand touts its whole grains, protein, and fiber, and upgraded ingredients.

FUN FACT: Initially, the brand was represented by two animated mascots, BJ the penguin and the Chef, a cartoon bear. Soon, the Chef was phased out, and BJ the penguin was replaced by KC, a different, hipper penguin that apparently enjoys snowboarding, hockey, and—for some reason—breakdancing.

Kindergarten Cop

Quick—how many times have you seen *Kindergarten Cop*? If your answer is anything less than eight thousand, either you grew up on Uranus or you're lying. Thank you very much, every basic cable station ever. It's on twenty-four-seven for good reason: The 1990 flick is an irresistible blend of cute kids ("Boys have a penis; girls have a vagina," one bright tyke informs the class) and Ahnold Schwarzenegger one-liners ("Thanks foah da tip," he deadpans in response). It's the movie that taught us that the future Governator could play characters other than thick-necked, thick-accented barbarians. He could also play thick-necked, thick-accented undercover cops!

The plot: Tough-guy Schwarzenegger goes undercover as a teacher in Oregon to catch a drug dealer. The draw is watching the former bodybuilder deliver lines like "Who is yoah daddy and what does he do?" "I'm da pahty poopah," and the most Arnoldiest line of all time: "It's not a toomah."

Ahnold's experience with whiny, nap-needing kindergarteners likely came in handy when he moved into the California governor's office and had to deal with politicians all day.

STATUS: Still all over the airwaves—on TBS, TNT, USA, CMT . . .

FUN FACT: The penis-vagina kid, Miko Hughes, also played the blonde zombie toddler who sawed though Herman Munster's heel in *Pet Sematary*.

Koosh Balls

In the late '80s, Koosh balls became the latest gotta-have-it craze, like Slinkys and Pet Rocks before them. The multicolored balls were an explosion of flexible strings protruding from a soft core—a rubber-scented sea urchin. And unlike their underwater cousins, you could fling a Koosh across the room without worrying about impaling someone in the eye or breaking a tooth.

They were simple to catch, but if you did bobble one, you didn't have to chase it under the couch. Unlike most balls, they couldn't roll. When they landed, the little pom-poms would settle into the ground with a rustle and a sigh, and wait for you to pick them up. While they were great for tossing, Kooshes were even better for absently—and addictively—picking at. You'd pull at the individual threads and they'd snap back like rainbow-colored whips.

We couldn't fight it, nor did we want to: Kooshmania had

taken hold, and expanded into everything from key chains to yo-yos. In 1990, the manufacturer even anthropomorphized the things by introducing Koosh Kins, with plastic heads, hands, and feet. They looked like little rubber Chia pets, and even had their own comic-book series. Your move, Pet Rock.

STATUS: Still around.

FUN FACT: Rosie O'Donnell regularly launched Kooshes at the camera and into the audience during her late-'90s talk show.

Kris Kross

Here are ten little words that may make you want to jump, jump off a bridge: The kids from Kris Kross are now in their thirties. Can that even be possible? It doesn't get more wiggedy-wiggedy-wiggedy wack than that.

Depending on your perspective, Kris Kross was either a talented kajillion-selling rap duo, or two little kids with their pants on backward. But whatever you thought of thirteen-year-old Chris "Mac Daddy" Kelly and Chris "Daddy Mac" Smith, who hopped around with preteen swagger and looked like they got dressed in the dark, you couldn't ignore their 1992 double-platinum single, "Jump." The tune sprang to the top of the Billboard Hot 100 charts and stayed there for eight weeks, and the little guys reared their cutie-pie heads on uber-'90s shows like *In Living Color* and *A*

Different World. Why? Well, they were even more adorable than a pair of hip-hop kittens and pumped up the jams better than rappers twice their age.

So was their smash hit in-depth social commentary about breaking the rules and doing their own thing, or just a frothy ode to leaping into the air? Yeah, probably the second one. One of their follow-up songs was about missing the bus.

STATUS: The duo has been replaced by other just-beyond-babies with microphones, notably Justin Bieber.

FUN FACT: Kris Kross probably played a lot of video games, but they weren't great at inspiring them. *Electronic Gaming Monthly* named the duo's video game to its list of the twenty worst of all time.

Lamb Chop's Play Along

Preschoolers who watched *Lamb Chop's Play Along* from 1992 to 1997 had no idea that Emmy-winning puppeteer Shari Lewis and her goofy puppets had also delighted their parents' generation back in the 1960s and 1970s. They just knew that the curly-headed lady in overalls and shiny neon shirts had a delightfully wacky way of entertaining them, like a beloved grandma who was always slightly off her meds.

Lewis brought her classic puppets to the show, including sweet little Lamb Chop, and frolicked with a rainbow connection of kids who were blatantly not actors. The show taught lessons (Lamb Chop negotiated for a raise in her penny a week allowance), but really revolved around Shari's songs. They ranged from rollicking and goofy ("Cat Wearing a Hat") to sweet and touching ("If You Should Run Away") to the most indelibly memorable of the group, "The Song That Never Ends" ("it just goes on and on, my friends . . ."). *Aaugh, make it stop!*

Just as the Neighborhood of Make-Believe wouldn't have existed but for Fred Rogers, so Shari Lewis's personal charisma cast the spell that made *Lamb Chop's* magic work. In 1998, the show spun off into a new program, *Charlie Horse Music Pizza*, but that was canceled when Lewis died of uterine cancer that same year. The song that never ends, it turns out, must now replay its happy insanity only in beloved childhood memories.

STATUS: Daughter Mallory continues to perform with her mom's most famed character, Lamb Chop.

FUN FACT: Shari Lewis and her husband wrote an episode of the original *Star Trek* in 1968. Beam me up, Lamb Chop.

Leisure Suit Larry

The Leisure Suit Larry series was to computer games what *Porky's* was to movies—goofy, sometimes groaningly bad sex jokes loosely holding a story together. Not the most mature entertainment out there, but a heaping helping of lowbrow fun.

Larry was Larry Laffer, a nerdy wannabe womanizer in a white leisure suit who looked and acted a little like Jack's horny best friend (also named Larry!) on *Three's Company*. He wasn't out to shoot zombies or win football games—Larry's entire goal was to slip between the sheets with any female he met.

It wasn't so easy for poor Lar. He needed to find passwords on restroom walls, avoid spoiled spinach dip, bribe drunks with wine, and dodge the KGB. But there was a sweet charm to the lovable loser, and the saucy scenes and double entendres felt fresh and even naughty. The games were like the first dirty joke you heard: not really that dirty, not really that funny, but always fondly remembered.

STATUS: In 2009, *Leisure Suit Larry: Box Office Bust* was released, focusing on Larry's nephew. Critics hated it. Larry's creator, Al Lowe, was not involved with this game or the one preceding it.

FUN FACT: The original games used an age-verification quiz to see if players were old enough to play such a risqué offering. Players had to identify Spiro Agnew or know Annette Funicello's last name in order to be allowed to play.

Light-Up Sneakers

Move over, cure for cancer: In the '90s, the world's greatest researchers focused their efforts on something even more important: shoes that lit up.

Talk about a bright idea. Kids understood that anything was

better when it glowed in the dark. And at first, children were the most fervent customers. They simply *had* to have princess-pink shoes that exploded into a seizure-inducing light show, or sleek black sneakers with flickering red lights in the heel that pulsed with every step, stuttering and flickering like epileptic fireflies. Eventually, bling-wearing adults were drawn to the footwear like moths to a battery-operated flame, spending big bucks on basketball shoes that would light up when the player's feet left the ground and running shoes designed to keep nighttime joggers from getting hit by a bus.

Creative people found other uses for the frenetic footwear, like helping you find your seat after the movie started, or kicking at the front door after dark so you could fit your key in the lock. As long as we had our sneakers, we never had to carry a flashlight again.

STATUS: After environmental watchdogs banned the shoes for using mercury in the lighting mechanism, light-up shoes made a comeback without it.

FUN FACT: Ever wonder why the human species hasn't lived up to its potential? In a 2001 interview, comedian George Carlin blamed people's obsession with light-up sneakers, Salad-Shooters, and DustBusters.

The Lion King

Remember when Benson voiced a baboon, Ferris Bueller played a lion, and Darth Vader was his fa-thaaaah? In 1993's blockbuster *The Lion King*, Robert Guillaume, Matthew Broderick, and James Earl Jones led an all-star voice cast in a classic animated tale of death, darkness, and fart jokes.

Even though it was rated G, *The Lion King* was much more adult-themed than bouncy, Elton John–penned tunes like "Hakuna Matata" initially made it seem. It tapped into common fears all kids had, like losing a parent and getting trampled by wildebeests.

With his slinky prowl and slithery speech, baddie Scar (Jeremy Irons, at his creepiest) ranks right up there with Cruella de Vil and *Snow White*'s Evil Queen as the most terrifying Disney villains ever drawn. And (spoiler alert) Mufasa's death packed an emotional wallop equal only to Bambi's mom becoming a rec-room trophy. Parents always die in Disney films, but in *The Lion King*, little cub Simba was even blamed for his beloved dad's demise. "No worries for the rest of your days"? For kids in the audience, it was more like "tortuous nightmares every time mom turned out the light." *The Lion King* taught a generation of American children that "the circle of life" was nothing to mess around with.

STATUS: The movie gave birth to two direct-to-video sequels and a TV show. As successful as the original film was, the "hairy *Hamlet*" concept took on an even bigger life three years later when it was reborn as a Broadway musical. The puppet-heavy production gave the story a depth and weight that made the cartoon seem, well, two-dimensional.

FUN FACT: *The Lion King* marked the second time that James Earl Jones and Madge Sinclair, who voiced Simba's parents, teamed up as an African king and queen. The first time was as Eddie Murphy's mom and dad in 1988's *Coming to America*.

Lisa Frank School Supplies

Panda bears juggling paintbrushes. Penguins perching on rainbows. Bunnies dancing ballet. Puppies sniffing starfish on the beach. Kittens snuggled into giant sneakers. And all of it was drenched in rainbows, as if a clown had sneezed. If it involved a cute baby animal and a helluva lot of bright colors, you could probably find it on a Lisa Frank folder.

Lisa Frank was around in the 1980s too, but it was in the 1990s that she really ruled the kingdom of cool school supplies. From folders to pencils, backpacks to book covers, her acid-trippy, neon-bright designs were everywhere. It was like an animated unicorn ate a rainbow and barfed all over America's junior high lockers.

STATUS: In 2011, Lisa Frank began selling clothing. There's also an iPhone app, Lisa Frank Pic n' Share, which allows users to Lisa Frankify their own photographs with her colorful characters.

FUN FACT: Yes, Lisa Frank is a real person, and to no one's surprise, she loves color. Her sons are named Hunter Green and Forrest Green, and she told the *Daily* in 2012 that "my house really is purple. And yellow and hot pink and light green and orange."

Mac Classic II

While many '90s kids got their first taste of home computers by banging around with their older siblings' Commodore 64s or TRS-80s, it was the Mac Classic II that created a generation of gadget addicts. Born with the decade in 1990, this was the first Mac for the masses. It had personality—and had us salivating at the prospect of a future filled with sleekly designed,

whimsical robots that lived on our desktops and did our home-work while we grabbed a quick nap.

Because the Mac Classic II was relatively affordable (around one thousand dollars), the little guy showed up en masse in classrooms from coast to coast, and quickly became the coolest dude in school. We didn't care that it was a cutting-edge educational tool—we just wanted to be friends with it. We could play games (*Stunt Copter! Lode Runner!*). We could change the system sounds, from *bink-bonk* to *boiiinnngg*. We could even make it swear, thanks to the speech synthesizer. Did every kid make their Mac utter the famous line from *WarGames*, "Shall we play a game?" or was it just us?

The fact that it had a nearly microscopic nine-inch, black-and-white screen was beside the point. We had Apples in our eyes, and could taste the juicy, gadget-filled future.

STATUS: It birthed a generation of Apple devotees, who gobbled up everything else the iCompany ever iMade.

FUN FACT: When the Mac Classic II crashed, it played the infamous "chimes of death," and showed an image of the "sad Mac," with Xs for eyes and a frowny face.

"Macarena"

Trying to remember exactly how long Aunt Julie and Uncle Steve have been married? If you remember doing the Macarena at their wedding, they almost certainly wed in 1995 or 1996, when the loopiest dance this side of the Hokey Pokey held America in its thrall. Part country line dance, part calisthenics, and a little bit follow-the-leader, the dance and its thudding earworm of a song were as ubiquitous at mid-'90s nuptials as Jordan almonds and drunk cousins.

Nobody ever knew the words and half of them were in Spanish anyway. It didn't matter. All you did was stand next to Grandma Bev and try to follow along, hopping here, slapping your palm out there, grabbing your neck when everyone else did, and randomly chiming in on "Hey! Macarena!" The smart dancers would time their hopping and twisting to get them over closer to the bar to grab a G&T and a chair before "Achy Breaky Heart" started up.

STATUS: You can still dig up recordings of the song of course, but it's not a wedding-reception staple anymore. Dearly beloved, we are awfully thankful for that.

FUN FACT: Matthew Wilkening of AOL Radio offered these simple instructions on how to Macarena: "First: Place your arm straight out in front of you at shoulder height, palm facing down. Then: Punch the DJ."

Magic Eye Pictures

Oh, the '90s—what other decade could have launched a craze where you just stand there and stare? Magic Eye images were everywhere—from books to mousepads to neckties. With so many people contorting their eyeballs, it's a wonder Visine's stock didn't go through the roof.

Magic Eye was 3-D without red-and-blue glasses—all you had to do was relax your eyes and look "through" the image, and all of a sudden it'd come into focus: A jumble of stars would melt away and reveal a hidden picture of Saturn. Or a bunch of cereal logos would turn into a dinosaur (yes, this really happened—on the back of a box of Honey Nut Cheerios).

Hit any mall in the early '90s, and you'd see groups of people from all walks of life huddled around a poster kiosk, staring at a picture in slack-jawed silence. Eventually, someone would exclaim, "I see it!" like they won the eyeball lottery and then stand there smugly gloating. ("He can't see it. Can you believe it? What a tool.") Eventually, most people would get it. But there was always that one kid who couldn't see the picture, no matter how hard he strained. And after his friends had all seen the hidden sailboat and were getting antsy to go to Orange Julius, he suddenly lied and exclaimed, "Oh, *there* it is." It was obvious he still couldn't get it, but everybody just believed him, because hey, Orange Julius.

STATUS: A Magic Eye 3-D puzzle still runs in newspaper comic sections across the country.

FUN FACT: In 1995's *Mallrats*, Ethan Suplee's character spends a good portion of the movie struggling to see a sailboat in a Magic Eye poster.

Magic Middles Cookies

The Keebler Elves seem awfully industrious for tiny critters who live in a tree. In the late 1980s and early 1990s, they came up with one of their best inventions yet, the short-lived Magic Middles cookies. Why frost a cookie in the normal spot, the top, when you can shake things up by cramming the frosting inside instead? These shortbread cookies looked boring and plain on the outside, but one chomp bathed your tastebuds in icing heaven.

In the commercial, an Einstein-looking mad scientist elf danced around yelling about what "genius" the cookies were. And he was right, but like many acts of genius, the Magic Middles weren't appreciated in their own time. They fell off the Keebler tree for good by the middle of the decade. Only an IV hooked up between your mouth and a can of frosting could replace their gooey-liciousness now.

STATUS: They're all gone. But Pepperidge Farm Milano Melts are similar, if way more expensive, and not elf-baked.

FUN FACT: The late Danny Dark, whose distinctive voiceover is heard in Keebler commercials, also provided the voice of Superman in Hanna-Barbera's *Super Friends*.

Martha Stewart

There is nothing simple that Martha Stewart cannot make headache-inducingly complicated. The rest of us squash together a s'more from store-bought supplies; Martha crafts homemade marshmallows and chocolate and hand whittles a stick. The rest of us order a pizza; Martha cures her own pepperoni and whips up artisan cheese.

Want to know just how removed Martha was from the rest of us? Check out her monthly calendar in *Martha Stewart Living* magazine. You might think you were doing well if you remembered to make a dental appointment or walk the dog, but Martha's calendar included items such as "Have beehives inspected" and "Replace winter doormats."

But her perfection hypnotized us. From her magazine to her TV show to her Kmart (Kmart!) products, the 1990s were Martha's era. Few thought they could match her, with her eight-page cake recipes and her hazelnut brittle wrapped in gold leaf, but it was tough not to admire her. You might not want to be her, but you sure wouldn't mind being invited to one of her parties.

STATUS: Martha now runs several empires, from media to furniture.

FUN FACT: Martha told Howard Stern that she broke up with Sir Anthony Hopkins because she couldn't stop thinking of him as Hannibal Lecter. Too bad. We're guessing she could have whipped up something pretty spectacular with fava beans and a nice Chianti.

MC Hammer

Just when we thought the national nightmare known as parachute pants was tucked back into our collective bottom drawer, in shuffled MC Hammer. Decked out in a wispy 'stache and chemistry-teacher glasses, the rapper became an instant pop-culture phenomenon with his 1990 smash hit "U Can't Touch This," which combined the hook from Rick James's "Super Freak" with sideways-shuffling dance moves and those infamous baggy drawers. He looked like a pop-rap crab.

Hammer's clean-cut image sparked backlash from more

hard-core rappers, but they couldn't touch his ability to connect with the masses, who clamored for Hammer dolls, school supplies, even a Saturday-morning cartoon. And the pants. Oh, the pants! Cinched on the top and bottom, his low-crotched, billowy trousers were part giant garbage bag, part genie outfit. The pants were perfect for granting someone three wishes or—with their gigantic pockets—stealing shrimp from a buffet. Maybe because his legs were scuttling so fast in the video, we didn't understand just how ridiculous the outfit looked at the time. We do now.

STATUS: Hammer—real name: Stanley Burrell—is apparently too legit to quit: After declaring bankruptcy in 1996, he appeared on the first season of *The Surreal Life* in 2003, and officiated at Corey Feldman's wedding. Today, Hammer is a web mogul who manages mixed–martial arts fighters and has more than 2.5 million Twitter followers.

FUN FACT: He reportedly earned the nickname Hammer from baseball star Reggie Jackson after spending years working as a batboy for the Oakland A's. Mr. October thought he looked like Hammerin' Hank Aaron.

McRib

What is it with McDonald's and limited-edition menu items? Does Ronald think he's running the Franklin Mint? At least the Shamrock Shake's seasonal availability makes sense, as the minty green drink is only available around St. Patrick's Day. But nothing explains the McRib. It's not like it only comes out for St. Porky's Day.

The weirdly shaped sandwich actually got its start in the 1980s, didn't do well, then returned and ruled in the 1990s. It was whisked away again in 2005 and now returns periodically, like a sauce-soaked Halley's Comet, to the delight of fans and the horror of foodies.

Even more than most McDonald's items, the McRib doesn't particularly seem to resemble food. Smashed into a boneless patty whose shape mimics a slab of ribs, then drenched in sauce and pickles and onions, its cult following boggles the mind. Perhaps it's made of pigs who were fed only crack doused in heroin gravy. Maybe one sandwich contains a magical golden chocolate-factory ticket. Those of us who refuse to try one may never know.

STATUS: The McRib gives McDonald's a sweet little limited-edition sales buzz every time they bring it back, so it will surely keep returning for periodic sauce-slopping visits.

FUN FACT: In a *Simpsons* episode, Homer becomes addicted to Krusty Burger's Ribwich. When someone asks if the meat comes from a pig, Krusty the Clown responds, "Think smaller, and more legs."

Melrose Place

When *Melrose Place* spun off from *Beverly Hills, 90210* in 1992, it was a completely standard drama. The plotlines surrounding a bunch of good-looking twentysomethings living together in an L.A. apartment complex were boring and trite (Jane loses her wedding ring!) and always wrapped up in sixty minutes.

Enter Special Guest Star for Life Heather Locklear, who bought the building and proceeded to make more than one cast member's life hell. Finally, the writers realized *Melrose* wasn't an After-School Special, it was a nighttime soap, and the catfights started to fly. Kimberly ripping off her wig to reveal a horribly scarred head became one of the most shocking moments of 1990s television.

From then on, it was all stolen babies, stalkers, canceled weddings, and eventually the entire apartment building being blown up. Turns out you don't need to have *Dynasty*-sized shoulder pads or *Dallas* oil money to board an E-ticket tide to Crazyland.

STATUS: After being canceled in 1999, *Melrose Place* was brought back on the CW network in 2009, but was yanked after one season.

FUN FACT: The El Pueblo Apartments in the Los Feliz neighborhood of Los Angeles stood in for the exterior of the Melrose Place apartment building, but the real apartments had no pool—that was built on a soundstage.

Mentos

What in blazes do they put in Mentos anyway? Insane problem-solving powder?

The commercials for the tubes of tasty mints all set up some weirdly minor dilemma and created equally bizarre homespun solutions. The woman whose car was hemmed in popped a Mentos and magically conjured up four hunky, overall-clad workmen who lifted the car out of its cramped parking space. The guy who sat on a freshly painted bench rolled around to pinstripe his whole suit. The woman who broke a heel on her shoe snapped off the other heel to even out the pair.

Not only were the skits strange, but the overwhelmingly happy actors appeared to have been plucked from the reject bin at a community-college theater department. Even the theme song didn't make sense. "Fresh goes better!" Fresh what? Where is it going? Is this even a place we want to go to?

And then, things became clear. "*Men-tos!* The *fresh*-maker!" crowed an unidentifiable-yet-definitely accented voice. So . . . these little skits were high comedy to people in Europe? New Zealand? South Africa? There was definitely some cultural chasm that we were incapable of crossing here, but the ads' campiness did its job. As far as poppable candy went, we may have preferred Life Savers, but everyone we know sampled a Mentos at least once. And yet our random parking and wardrobe problems remained unsolved. Who do we sue for false advertising?

STATUS: Available everywhere.

FUN FACT: In 1999, a chemistry professor demonstrated how dropping Mentos into carbonated soda creates an Old Faithful–like geyser effect, and bored people with video cameras have been YouTubing the results ever since.

Micro Machines

E ver try to find a needle in a haystack? How about a Micro Machine dropped into your living room's shag carpet? Tracking down the teeny car was next to impossible—half the size of Hot Wheels, the ultra-miniature vehicles were extremely detailed, but you almost needed a jeweler's loupe or an electron microscope to play with them.

When we were able to see them, though, they were awesome. From planes, trains, and automobiles to campers, snowmobiles,

and farm equipment (not to mention *Star Wars*, *Star Trek*, and *Babylon 5* spaceships), Micro Machines and their working wheels let kids play benevolent transit god, crafting gigantic cities where the miniscule cars could vroom up and down ramps to their tiny hearts' content. The popular play sets doubled as storage bins, which was a good thing, since the vehicles were so small, we probably breathed in a few loose ones.

STATUS: The Micro Machines brand ran out of gas after Hasbro bought it in 1999, but the tiny-vehicle concept remains wildly popular, from microscopic *Star Wars* spaceships to pintsized Captain America motorcycles.

FUN FACT: The guy in the TV commercials, John Moschitta Jr., was in the Guinness Book of World Records as the world's fastest talker. ("ThisistheMicroMachineManpresentingthemostmidgetminiaturemotorcadeofMicroMachines.")

Mighty Morphin Power Rangers

*M*ighty *Morphin Power Rangers* was the story of five teenagers who lived in California, but always seemed to fight their battles in Japan. No wonder, since the show used a Zord-load of footage that had already aired in Asia. Didn't matter, though. American kids couldn't get enough of watching the Rangers

leap and flip through the air like color-coordinated Mary Lou Rettons, kicking at the Putty Patrol, clay-faced baddies who scarily resembled the Sleestaks from *Land of the Lost* days.

When they slipped into their brightly hued tights and helmets—which, for some reason, had unsettling plastic lips—the Rangers couldn't go two seconds without making exaggerated arm movements and striking poses like Madonna on the cover of *Vogue*. Yeah, they were agile and flippy, but their coolest ability was being able to pilot their Dinozords, robot vehicles modeled after prehistoric animals. When giant monsters showed up, which was always, the Power Rangers could combine their Zords into a humongous Megazord. Go, go, Power Rangers! Not so cool: They ended up making the Asian girl the Yellow Ranger and the black guy the Black Ranger. Color this show a little bit racist.

STATUS: The show transformed into two movies, and the franchise keeps on morphin' into new series. The original Rangers are now in their forties.

FUN FACT: The Power Rangers were such a phenomenon that celebrities like Mike Myers and Gene Simmons from Kiss would stop by the set.

Milli Vanilli

Girl, you know it's true: Milli Vanilli was one of the most popular musical acts of the '90s—with an accent on the "act." With their slightly vacant expressions, spandex outfits, humongous shoulder pads, and tightly woven dreadlocks, Fab Morvan and Rob Pilatus shot to international stardom, taking home the Grammy for Best New Artist in 1990.

They probably should have won an Oscar too, because it soon came out that the photogenic duo didn't actually sing a note on their album. Like Greg Brady's Johnny Bravo, they fit the suits. Everybody involved rushed to point fingers, and media, audiences, and their record label revolted. Who was really at fault for the Milli Vanilli scandal? Blame it on the rain.

Say what you will about their lip-synching—and truth-telling—abilities, but you've got to admit the model-slash-dancers were the pioneers of some very specific sweet moves, including the slow-motion-hair-spin, the in-air-chest-bump, and the run-in-place. In 1993, Rob and Fab released an album that they did actually sing on, but it flopped. Buh-ba-ba-bye, baby.

STATUS: Milli Vanilli is no more—Pilatus died of a suspected drug overdose in 2008—but talk of a big-screen biopic persists.

FUN FACT: At least they had a sense of humor about their downfall. Rob and Fab starred in a 1991 commercial for Carefree sugarless gum. The concept was that the gum's flavor would last until the two actually sang for themselves.

"MMMBop"

Everybody's ears perked up the first time they heard "MMMBop," the jaunty, jangly 1997 tune by Hanson, the family band made up of two brothers and their cute sister. What, Taylor was actually a boy? Well, by that point, who cared? The song and its nonsense chorus was everywhere—a blond-headed earworm. It hit number one in twenty-seven countries and was so sugary, it surely caused thousands of cavities. The lyrics gave the world deep thoughts to ponder, like "Mmmbop, ba duba dop, ba du bop . . . Yeah."

"MMMBop" backlash reached a fever pitch in 2005 when a high school in Pennsylvania used it to raise money for the victims of Hurricane Katrina, playing it on the school loudspeaker until students and teachers kicked in three thousand dollars. The "Stop the Bop" fund-raiser quickly hit its goal, and Hanson ended up matching the funds. The fact that Isaac, Zac, and Taylor were in on the joke and even today aren't taking great pains to distance themselves from their biggest hit makes us dig them even more. The capper: In 2011, they announced plans to release a beer called . . . wait for it . . . MMMhop. Sounds like the eternally pre-teen (in our minds, anyway) brothers finally found a way to get into bars.

STATUS: Still MMMBopping along. Hansen launched a well-received album in 2010, and continues to tour all over the world, performing "MMMBop" in a lower key—now that they finally made it through puberty.

FUN FACT: *Rolling Stone* named "MMMBop" the sixth-worst song of the '90s.

Movie Rental Stores

In the early days, your parents had to leave a ginormous deposit in order to lug an equally ginormous VCR home, because no one actually owned one. Then they had to wrangle with the cords and somehow hook it up to your TV, all to rent something lame like *Savannah Smiles* for your tenth birthday party.

But when the video-store industry settled into its stride, oh, the places you'd go. You could walk out with an eclectic triple-feature of *Slumber Party Massacre, Honey, I Shrunk the Kids,* and *Lethal Weapon 2* all under your arm! And movie stores immediately turned into one-stop shops. Who knew those purse-sized packs of Raisinets and bizarre offerings like Sno-Caps and Goobers existed outside of a theater's shiny glass case? If your video store was diverse enough, you could even snag a tanning session before you left. Be kind, rewind!

But the high life for movie-rental stores was a short one. VHS tapes were replaced by DVDs, and the craze for wandering the aisles, then having to return the movie the next day, started to wane. Choosing from a streaming website or opening a Netflix envelope was so much easier. Movie stores started a fight for life to rival anything in a Bette Midler–starring tearjerker. But, while it lasted, what a show it was.

STATUS: Many brick-and-mortar stores were shuttered when Netflix and Amazon streaming came to town.

FUN FACT: Acclaimed movie director Quentin Tarantino worked at a southern California video store called Video Archives for years, and says the discussion of film sparked by his job helped lead to his career.

Movies with Twist Endings

You could argue that 1941's *Citizen Kane* was where the cinematic twist ending was born (ahem, Rosebud), but the film world's zig-zig-zig-*zag*! gimmick really took hold in the '90s. For a while, you couldn't step into a multiplex without getting the Jujube-covered rug pulled out from under you just before the credits ran.

The Crying Game was one of the first to really capitalize on its "wait . . . *what*?!" left turn. (Spoiler: Dude looks like a lady.) *Seven*, *Fight Club*, and *Primal Fear* all used sleight-of-hand to misdirect, and then delivered a dizzying punch to the head while moviegoers were looking the other direction. One of the best twists ever came courtesy of 1995's *The Usual Suspects*. We won't ruin it for you, but it turns out that Kevin Spacey's seemingly harmless nerd is actually the big bad Keyzer Soze. Wait—well, I guess we will ruin it for you. Sorry.

Perhaps the most famous fake-out was served up in 1999's *The*

Sixth Sense, where Haley Joel Osment sees dead people—like Bruce Willis. Director M. Night Shyamalan rode that "surprise, suckas!" wave well into the 2000s, where he finally fizzled after producing critically drubbed fare like *The Happening*, where Marky Mark tried to talk a plant out of taking over the world. You mean you can't base an entire career on jerking the audience around? What a twist!

STATUS: Just about every horror flick these days tacks on a surprise at the end.

FUN FACT: The famous *Sixth Sense* quote became one of movie-dom's most parodied. In one opening scene for a *Simpsons* episode, Bart writes on the school chalkboard, "I can't see dead people."

My So-Called Life

The *L.A. Times* once wrote that *My So-Called Life* was "*Beverly Hills, 90210* minus the lobotomy." Angsty Angela Chase (a luminous Claire Danes) wouldn't have known how to deal with Brenda and Brandon and their bikini-clad, Jaguar-driving friends. To her, school was like a drive-by shooting, where you're just lucky to get out alive.

Angela was battling to find herself—dying her hair red, leaving good-girl friend Sharon behind, crushing desperately on soulful-looking Jordan Catalano, and dabbling in the daring world of new pals Rayanne Graff and Rickie Vasquez. In the all-consuming world that is high school, she was suddenly sure she didn't measure up, and finding out was agony.

Created by veterans of *Thirtysomething*, *MSCL* lasted just one short year, but that was enough to forever cement it in the minds of those who found the small truths of growing up in boxes of hair dye, band practice, and love letters never sent.

STATUS: The show ended in 1995, after just one season. *Gilmore Girls* attracted similar devotion in the 2000s, though Lorelai and Rory's sisterly relationship was one Patty Chase could only dream of having with Angela.

FUN FACT: In the 2008 film *Juno*, screenwriter Diablo Cody inserted a reference to never-seen Tino from Jordan Catalano's band, Frozen Embryos.

Mystery Science Theater 3000

The nineties were the decade that overlaid commentary onto everything. *Beavis and Butt-Head* and *Pop Up Video* mocked music videos and *Talk Soup* took jabs at talk shows, but no one did the supplementary soundtrack better than *Mystery Science Theater 3000*.

You know the story: In the not-too-distant future, a human (first

Joel, then Mike) is imprisoned in space with wisecracking robots Tom Servo, Crow T. Robot, and sometimes Gypsy, and forced to watch bad movies and equally awful mental hygiene shorts.

A great idea turned golden. How else would the world have discovered *Manos: The Hands of Fate*, a film made by a fertilizer salesman? Or met up with chubby Canadian ex-cult member Zap Rowsdower, the supposed hero of *The Final Sacrifice*? Or watched victims in 1964's *The Creeping Terror* helpfully crawl into the monster's mouth?

Some viewers were Joel diehards, others preferred Mike's riffs. Some loved the team of Dr. Forrester and TV's Frank, others got a kick out of Pearl, Bobo, and Observer. But whatever your favorite player on the ever-changing roster, this was and remains the all-star team of commentary comedy.

STATUS: *MST3K* alums have formed two similar movie-mocking groups, RiffTrax and Cinematic Titanic.

FUN FACT: Joel, Mike, and the bots are stuck on the *Satellite of Love*, which takes its name from the 1972 Lou Reed song.

Nelson

Those dainty, dollish features. Those pouty lips. Those long, golden locks. Nope, not Malibu Barbie: We're talking about Matthew and Gunnar Nelson, the twin brothers who rocked '90s audiences' socks off to the tune of more than six and a half million albums. Never has there been a more literal representation of the term "hair band."

Armed with a unique acoustic-meets-electric sound and catchy harmonies—and, we're guessing, industrial-size vats of Pantene stashed in the tour bus—the Teutonic-looking twins took over MTV with hits like "(Can't Live Without Your) Love and Affection" and "After the Rain."

With platinum, California-girl, corn-silk hair down to their waists, the brothers looked a little like they could be the spawn of Edgar Winter, but their musical family tree was actually even more impressive. With '40s-and-'50s TV icons Ozzie and Harriet Nelson for grandparents, and rocker Ricky Nelson for a dad, entertainment—along with a gene for lady hair—was woven into their DNA. Today, with their Samson-esque locks finally chopped, they look more like the twins from *The Suite Life of Zack & Cody* than dolls you just wanted to brush.

STATUS: The brothers tour more than one hundred dates a year, both as Nelson, and as a Ricky Nelson tribute band.

FUN FACT: Matthew and Gunnar's sister, Tracy Nelson, is an actress best known for playing crime-solving Sister Steve, the sidekick of Tom Bosley's Father Dowling character.

Nerf Guns

Pew! Pew! From cowboy six-shooters to rat-a-tat Tommy guns to outer-space lasers, kids from every generation have played with faux firearms. But Nerf made the first toy weapons that let Billy shoot his little brother right in the face.

Sure, they were loaded with foam projectiles, not real ammo, but still. In the '90s, Nerf came out with marketing barrels a-blazing, unleashing its "Nerf or nothin'!" campaign. The commercials made it clear that you needed to beg your mom to buy a bunch of newfangled Nerf weapons or you'd be ganged up on by every kid in the neighborhood and pelted to within an inch of your unarmed life. Millions of Nerf-less kids feigned the flu so they wouldn't be stalked and gunned down with foam bullets while they were waiting for the bus.

The brightly colored Nerf weapons lived up to the hype—Arrowstorm, semiautomatics with rotating turrets loaded with foam arrows; Ballzooka, which let you unleash a constant storm of round bullets; and the Nerf Slingshot, with its TV commercial featuring a street-talkin' Seth Green unleashing holy hell in a shopping mall. In those pre-9/11 days, it was perfectly acceptable to carry loaded weapons in public and shoot mimes—which Green inexplicably did. Of course, today, he'd be Tased by mall security and sent to Guantanamo.

STATUS: Today's Nerf guns feature tech even the CIA would admire, including glow-in-the-dark darts, removable clips, and electronic scopes.

FUN FACT: NERF originally stood for Non-Expanding Recreational Foam.

Newsies

Newsies seemed like it had everything going for it: The 1992 movie musical starred a seventeen-year-old Christian Bale as the leader of a ragtag group of singing newsboys; its rousing tunes were written by Alan Menken, who had just scored with *The Little Mermaid* and *Beauty and the Beast*; and it was directed by *Dirty Dancing* choreographer Kenny Ortega. Slam dunk, right? Wrong—*Newsies* didn't deliver: It ended up being one of the lowest-grossing movies in Disney history.

What in the name of Joseph Pulitzer happened? Critics identified the movie's glacial pace, labor-dispute plot, and terrible New Yawk accents as the reasons the film only raked in $3 million at the box office. Teenage fans who loved every note, leap, and fist pump didn't care that it was an extra!-extra!-huge flop, though, and theater geeks across the country made it their mission to win over new converts, passing along VHS copies and singing the movie's praises to anyone who would listen. Twenty years later, their campaign to give the flick a new life paid off: In 2012, *Newsies* finally made it to Broadway. See kids, it pays to recycle.

STATUS: Internet fervor for the flick continues, and the Broadway version opened to rave reviews. The real-life newspaper industry, on the other hand, is on life support.

FUN FACT: Max Casella, who played Racetrack Higgins in the movie, went on to originate the role of Timon the meerkat in the Broadway version of *The Lion King*.

The Nutty Professor

1996's *The Nutty Professor* was a retelling of the classic tale of Jekyll and Hyde, but with a lot more gravy. Oh, and also Eddie Murphy dressed as a woman, clapping and delightfully chanting, "Herc-a-lees, Herc-a-lees!"—something sadly missing from the 1963 original, where Jerry Lewis hammed it up as his buck-toothed "Hey, laaaady" character.

In the updated version, Murphy's four-hundred-pound college professor Sherman Klump drinks a potion that restructures his DNA, and transforms him into slick, slimmed-down swinger Buddy Love, also played by Murphy. Heck, nearly every character is played by Murphy, including his mom, dad, brother, grandma, and the Richard Simmons–looking exercise guru. And we wouldn't be surprised if he played Jada Pinkett too. That was the draw: The reason we kept buying tickets was to watch Murphy, Murphy, Murphy, and Murphy sitting around the dinner table together, handing each other fried chicken and farting.

The movie won an Oscar for Best Makeup, and kicked off a spate of actors in fat suits, notably Martin Lawrence in the eighteen *Big Momma* movies, Gwyneth Paltrow in *Shallow Hal*, and Mike Myers as Fat Bastard in the second and third *Austin Powers* flicks. Get in mah belly!

STATUS: Available on DVD. So is the 2000 sequel, *Nutty Professor II: The Klumps*.

FUN FACT: Even Murphy went back to the fat-suit well once again, this time as his own wife in 2007's *Norbit*.

OK Soda

Like Esperanto and yogurt-covered raisins, OK Soda was a cult invention that some people loved with a passion, but that never really caught on with everybody. In 1993, beverage giant

Coca-Cola looked at Generation X's reputation as sullen slackers, and decided that even brooding layabouts bought pop. And so they rolled out the most noncorporate corporate beverage ever, OK Soda.

The cans, designed by alt cartoonists Daniel Clowes and Charles Burns, featured a gray-and-black motif and startlingly bleak designs. The flavor was kind of like fruity Fresca, but kids raised with free rein at fountain-drink stands immediately recognized it as a "suicide," the drink you get when you mix a bit of each flavor offered into your cup. It's a SpriteFruitPunchLemonadeColaNanza!

It was an odd attempt to reach a generation that whatever its economic and internal struggles, still drank soda like pretty much everyone else in the nation. By 1995, OK was KO'd.

STATUS: It's been replaced by boutique sodas like Jones Soda, with flavors like Turkey & Gravy for Thanksgiving and Latke for Hanukkah.

FUN FACT: OK had a hotline where people could leave random messages, and a manifesto, parts of which ("What's the point of OK? Well, what's the point of anything?") were printed on the cans.

The Olsen Twins

While most nine-month-olds were pooping in their nappies and blowing bubbles with their drool, Mary-Kate and Ashley Olsen were hitting their marks and probably demanding designer Similac for their dressing rooms. Starting in 1987, the tiny twosome took turns playing youngest moppet Michelle Tanner on ABC's *Full House*, delivering awww-inducing catchphrases ("You got it, dude!") and sending the show's cute rating off the charts.

The twins didn't get much bigger, but their careers—and bank accounts—sure did. They graduated to innocuous made-for-TV movies and hit the big screen with Kirstie Alley and Steve Guttenberg in the 1995 movie *It Takes Two*. The Olsens may have been pint-sized, but they became huge tween idols, released books, perfumes, and dolls, and even built a fashion empire. Mary-Kate is credited with starting the "bag lady" fashion trend, with her floppy hats, giant sunglasses, and enormous (for her) cardigans that looked like she found them in an alley.

In 2011, their clothing lines alone raked in more than a billion dollars. That's billion, with a "b." The fashion line started by their TV dad Bob Saget? Not so much. Okay, there wasn't really a Bob Saget fashion line, but we wish there was.

STATUS: Mary-Kate and Ashley have all but retired from acting, but they still manage to make headlines.

FUN FACT: In 2004, the sisters skipped their high school prom so they could host *Saturday Night Live*.

Online Services

Before the online world was everywhere, it was a private club. Membership required only a small monthly fee and the willingness to plunge in to untested technology waters before most people even knew how to dog paddle.

Whether you logged on via Prodigy, CompuServe, AOL, GEnie, or a similar offering, the procedure was pretty much the same. You could bounce around—at paint-dryingly grueling dial-up speed—to various forums, sharing recipes here, yacking about *Melrose Place* episodes there. You could shop, book travel, and check sports scores and stocks. For a world mostly without mobile phones and where many office computers still offered that horrible glowing green type on black backgrounds, this was a *Star Trek* level of futurism.

But the companies offering these services soon showed they had no real idea what they'd started. Prodigy, for one, expected to make money from its shopping options, and when it became apparent that users were gravitating instead to the friend-making and email functions, executives freaked out. The service tried to limit monthly messaging to thirty a month—a number most teens now routinely exceed before breakfast—and charge twenty-five cents for each additional message. But it was too late to save their business. We soon left online services behind, a quaint pair of water wings for a generation that was about to dive headlong into the technological deep end.

STATUS: The Internet's all just one big online service now, and everyone's on the same one.

FUN FACT: Actor Elwood Edwards, who voiced AOL's famous "You've got mail!" line, has parodied it many times, including "You've got hail!" for a weather forecast and "You've got leprosy!" for a *Simpsons* episode.

Oprah's Book Club

Oprah didn't exactly strike us as a hard-core reader. You didn't believe Ms. Winfrey was curling up with *Richard III* or Dostoyevsky in the original Russian. She probably owned a lot of Harlequins. But starting in 1996, the talk-show host became the publishing industry's BFF when she started Oprah's Book Club, choosing a new novel each month for her gazillions of viewers to buy and discuss.

And buy they did. If you worked at Waldenbooks or B. Dalton during the '90s or 2000s, Oprah was your nightmare. The second she announced her new title, the store phone lines lit up like the whole town was trying to win Bruce Springsteen tickets. Everyone wanted Oprah's pick, whether it was a classic like Elie Wiesel's *Night* or a newer favorite like Kaye Gibbons's *Ellen Foster*.

Oprah's club also resulted in some train-wrecky literary scandals. In the most famous, author James Frey was found to have made up parts of his supposed memoir, *A Million Little Pieces*, and had to come back on the show and try to explain his lies. In a quieter debacle, author Jonathan Franzen snubbed her pick of *The Corrections* in 2001 and felt the big O's resulting rage.

Of course, there were more than a few literary snobs who felt slapping an "Oprah's Book Club" sticker on a book's cover automatically made it uncool. But it's hard to argue with anything that gets the whole country reading. And the cash bump Oprah's attention created for her chosen authors was certainly more deserved than any paycheck MTV ever gave the cast of *Jersey Shore*.

STATUS: Oprah's Book Club ended with her syndicated show in 2011, but Winfrey restarted the club online, dubbing it "Oprah's Book Club 2.0," in 2012. Cheryl Strayed's *Wild* was her first pick.

FUN FACT: The only real flops among Oprah's choices were her final two. Charles Dickens's *Great Expectations* and *A Tale of Two Cities* never moved above number 52 on *USA Today*'s bestseller list. "Dickens let me down," Winfrey reportedly said.

Orbitz

People may not remember what Orbitz was called or how it tasted, but they remember how it looked. It was the drink that resembled a lava lamp, clear liquid in a curvaceous glass bottle with tiny colored balls bobbing inside.

Orbitz floated onto store shelves in 1997, in varieties that were less "flavors" and more "what happens when an entire produce section crashes into your beverage." Blueberry melon strawberry and pineapple banana cherry coconut were two of the choices, suggesting that someone in research and development had a bad case of option paralysis.

The flavors were weird, and the floating balls had no taste.

So really, the point of buying it was to look like you're drinking a lava lamp and to get to make a couple dozen "balls" jokes while you're at it. It's little wonder that the drink flopped within about a year, and an unrelated online travel agency took over its name.

STATUS: Asian bubble tea is becoming more popular, but the tapioca balls in it don't float, they settle to the bottom of the drink, to be sucked up through overly wide straws.

FUN FACT: One of the flavors was called "Charlie Brown Chocolate." We're seriously hoping Charles Schulz banked some royalties from that before Orbitz circled the drain.

The Oregon Trail

A fire hit your wagon! One of your oxen is injured! Inadequate grass! You have died of dysentery! What would you like on your tombstone? *The Oregon Trail*, one of the first computer games we were actually allowed to play in school, was no *Halo*, but heck if it wasn't stressful all on its own.

Who knew pioneer travel was all about budgeting, committing so much money for bullets versus so much for clothing? The math gave us a headache, but hey, we were getting out of class, so we played anyway. When allotting resources, we always tried to skimp on the food, but our greedy family insisted on adequate sustenance or punished us by keeling over. Oh, and never ford the damn river. Your wagon will break, your kids will drown, your food will float away.

Eh, forget it, Oregon's full of hippies and microbreweries anyway.

STATUS: The game's been updated many times and is now available on platforms that '80s and '90s kids couldn't even dream of, including iPhone and iPad.

FUN FACT: One spoof of the game reimagines it as *The Organ Trail*, and features a trek across a zombie-infested wasteland.

Pajama Pants

Who decided that pajama pants were an appropriate item of clothing to wear to school, shopping, or even church? Kids in the '90s, that's who. Part of the same comfort-trumps-fashion trend as that bizarre hospital-scrubs fad, flannel pj pants somehow became the must-have clothing item. It didn't matter that wearing them put you just one step away from throwing on a ratty terry-cloth bathrobe and matching slippers and shuffling into Social Studies with sleep drool still stuck to your cheek.

We're not sure what we were thinking—were we that lazy? Are the kids who wore plaid pajama bottoms to middle school the same adults who wear velour tracksuits to weddings? At least it never devolved into bringing a pillow and blankie to class, and sucking our thumbs during Calc.

But it did take an even weirder turn: Boxer shorts somehow became approved apparel. Girls (primarily) would show up for class adorned in flannel boxers, often with the fly sensibly sewn shut. Teachers must have been dumbstruck by their students' choice of bottom wear, which screamed "I'd rather be sleeping." Because nothing demonstrates a commitment to learning more than rolling out of bed and not bothering to change your pants.

STATUS: The debate over whether pajama pants are appropriate for school continues today. But it's all relative. Really, pajama bottoms are about the most innocuous dress-code worry parents and teachers face in this era of obscene T-shirts and sexy school outfits.

FUN FACT: The yellow dudes in the '90s kids' series *Bananas in Pajamas* wore pj's all day long, and nobody seemed to mind.

PalmPilot

Hey, you free for a movie on Thursday?" In the late 1990s, for the first time, the answer to that question was right in the palm of our hand. With the pint-sized PalmPilot PDA, introduced

in 1997, we no longer had to flip through our dictionary-sized day planner or—God forbid—run home and check our Garfield calendar to see if we were available.

It was easy as electronic pie: All you had to do was rummage around in your backpack until you found the little gizmo, flip open the plastic cover, wait for it to power up, use your fingernail to pry loose the stylus, tap the calendar icon, adjust the contrast wheel, squint to see the calendar and then curse when the screen suddenly went blank because you forgot to change the two double-A batteries that ran it. It was probably all moot, anyway, since you probably also forgot to sync the thing.

By the time you figured out if you were free, the movie you had planned to see had already been released on DVD.

STATUS: Today, personal digital assistants live in your smartphone, respond to verbal commands, and do everything but the dishes.

FUN FACT: *The Simpsons* loved to skewer the device: In one episode, mobster Fat Tony complains that his PalmPilot forgot to remind him about a meeting and that it needed to be "hot-synced." His henchman misunderstands and shoots it. ("You know how it is with us, everything means kill!") In another, Reverend Lovejoy's PDA is called a Psalm Pilot.

Party of Five

What kid hasn't had at least a fleeting thought about what life would be like if their parents suddenly disappeared? Sure, most imagine their newly orphaned life a la *Home Alone*, eating gobs of ice cream and tobogganing down the stairs. Too bad for the Salinger family it was a little more true-to-life on *Party of Five*, one of the most depressing shows ever to run on Fox, up to and including *When Animals Attack!*

The show was Lifetime-movie-heavy, as the five children tried to maneuver through life after their parents died in a car accident. Irresponsible Charlie, prodigy Claudia, confused Julia, Tom Cruise–y Bailey, and cipher Owen engendered a small but rabid group of fans, despite the fact that every other episode was about Bailey drinking again. That plotline was so frequent, it quickly became a pop-culture joke—like the episode of *Gilligan* where they almost got off the island.

Even though it often languished near the bottom of the ratings, *PO5* worked its way into watercooler buzz-dom by launching the careers of everybody from Neve Campbell to Jennifer Love Hewitt to Matthew Fox—before he became a purgatory-trapped ghost-angel-robot or whatever actually was going on during *Lost*. It may have starred a gaggle of soon-to-be-A-list celebs, but with its super-depressing plots, *Party of Five* wasn't all that much of a party.

STATUS: Reruns are hard to come by, but the party continues on DVD.

FUN FACT: An episode of *The X-Files* reportedly briefly shows the Salinger parents' gravestones in a cemetery scene.

Pogs

Pogs were more than a fad, they were approved gambling for kids! But gambling that might have been invented by an impatient third-grader with no athletic ability or desire to remember any rules. It was a game in the same way that hitting somebody with a stick and taking their stuff was a game.

First, you collected a ton of the little paper circles, which featured designs ranging from pro athletes to Hello Kitty to Batman to Bart Simpson. Stack them up along with some Pogs from your friend, and throw your slammer, a heavier playing piece, at the whole pile. Hey, did your throw send Joey's treasured Alf Pog faceup? Alf's furry little hide was yours now.

Grandma did it with jacks, Grandpa with marbles—but losing your favorite Pog still hurt like getting the wind knocked outta you in dodgeball. Nobody wanted to see their precious hologram

skull disappear into somebody else's grimy pocket. Sore losers—plus irresistible in-class trading—got the game banned from some schools. That was okay. By the time that the schools got around to cracking down, trends had shifted, and we would no sooner be seen with a tube of Pogs than we would wearing acid-washed jeans.

STATUS: The "collecting random tiny things in jillions of varieties" fad continues. Just ask a kid who loves Squinkies, Polly Pockets, or those cool food-shaped Japanese erasers.

FUN FACT: Pog stands for "passion fruit, orange, guava," and came from a Hawaiian drink whose bottle caps were reportedly first used to play the game.

Pokémon

In 1997, America was invaded by addictive little monsters that ate allowance money. American kids took the Pokémon slogan, "Gotta catch 'em all," literally, shelling out hundreds of dollars on trading cards aiming to score one of the rare valuable ones. Kids would collect, trade, and sell them with an obsessive frenzy, turning schools, playgrounds, and alleyways into pint-sized versions of the New York Stock Exchange. "Who's got a Bulbasaur? For the love of God, I need a Bulbasaur. Sell all the Squirtles! *Sell all the Squirtles!!*" Sadly, we've yet to meet a kid who was able to retire early because of his stash of Jigglypuff cards.

STATUS: Still massively popular, even though a group of parents filed a class-action lawsuit in 1999 that claimed that Pokémon cards were a form of illegal gambling and turning their kids into addicts.

FUN FACT: In 1999, Pikachu, the little yellow guy with a lightning-bolt tail, landed on the cover of *Time* magazine, which called him "the most famous mouse since Mickey and Mighty."

Pop Up Video

The 1990s were all about multitasking, and music videos were no exception. Why just veg out in front of an ordinary video when you could watch a video paired with *Beavis and Butt-Head* commentary or one adorned with *Pop Up Video*'s cartoony word bubbles?

The best pop-ups told you something hilarious, like the one on a Rick Astley video pointing out a dancer who never learned the steps, or confiding that the director and producer had a two-hour fight about whether Astley should roll up his sleeves. Awesomely, the writers of the pop-ups seemed to have the same bemused contempt for the music industry as the rest of us, never failing to point out where the producers cheaped out on a set or the singer was replaced with a stand-in.

Watching *Pop Up Video* was like kicking back with your friend who worked as the third director's assistant and letting him dish about the scene where Meat Loaf fell off his chair or snark that Dexys Midnight Runners fired their drummer midway through the shoot. The pop-ups were like musical footnotes, but footnotes that were often more entertaining than the real text.

STATUS: *Pop Up Video* popped off the air for a time in 2002, but was revived by VH1 in 2011.

FUN FACT: *Pop Up Brady* gave the pop-up treatment to old *Brady Bunch* episodes. One pop-up on the famed Kings' Island episode claims Robert Reed saved the cast's life by spotting a poorly mounted camera that would have flown off a roller coaster and possibly killed the actors.

Pretty Woman

Most prostitutes look more like "Pretty Woman" singer Roy Orbison than *Pretty Woman* star Julia Roberts, but when has a little thing like reality ever stopped the Hollywood movie dream machine?

In the 1990 smash-hit movie, tycoon Richard Gere hired reluctant escort Roberts, and they fell in love. Exactly like it always happens in real life! Awwww. It was a Cinderella story for a new generation, except instead of a glass slipper, she wore hooker boots. The romantic comedy sidestepped typical call-girl-movie issues, like jealous pimps and gonorrhea, and instead concentrated on the super-fun side of prostitution, like the slap-happy scene where Roberts let out a startled, hysterical "bwah-ha!" when Gere snaps a jewelry case on her gloved fingers. What was the next step in this odd courtship—slamming a car door on her thumb?

How does a flick about a prostitute's relationship problems appeal to a mass audience? Pretty well, apparently. The movie raked in almost $500 million worldwide. And the accompanying sound track went triple platinum, likely appealing to the skeezy guys who bought it because of Roberts and her thigh-high, black-leather boots on the cover, but also to preteens who thought Sweden's Roxette ("It Must Have Been Love") and their hairdos were rad.

STATUS: Available on DVD.

FUN FACT: Jason Alexander, *Seinfeld*'s George Costanza, costarred as a creep lawyer. Apparently, the jerk store called, and they were running out of him.

Pulp Fiction

Hey honey bunny, you know what they call the best movie of the '90s in France? They got the metric system there, so they call it—aw heck, they call it *Pulp Fiction*, just like we do.

Quentin Tarantino's 1994 hit shook up American audiences in a way that few films have since *Star Wars*. The one-time video-clerk-turned-director blended together humor, pop culture, shocking violence, and witty dialogue that stuck in your brain like a ball gag in a hapless boxer's mouth. From Samuel L. Jackson's pseudo-biblical quote to breakfasts of Big Kahuna burgers and Fruit Brute to the disturbing gimp in the pawnshop basement, this movie was a full-on fire hose aimed straight into the face of the Hollywood establishment.

Who knew John Travolta could make such a glorious comeback long after his Barbarino and disco-dancing days? Who knew film noir and brutal violence could go down as smoothly as a five-dollar milkshake? Who knew you could store a watch in such an uncomfortable spot? As Chuck Berry sang while Uma Thurman and Travolta twisted their hearts out at Jack Rabbit Slim's, it goes to show you never can tell.

STATUS: A whole generation of filmmakers learned from Tarantino that an independent film could be just as commercially and critically successful as a mainstream blockbuster.

FUN FACT: In the Big Kahuna scene Samuel L. Jackson tells John Travolta to "check out the big brain on Brad," even though the character's name is Brett.

The Real World

When *The Real World* began back in 1992, the middle word in the show's title wasn't actually laughable. Original cast members Julie, Andre, Eric, Kevin, Heather, Becky, and Norman were real—and they were also bright, inquisitive Gen Xers with varied backgrounds and actual career dreams. They argued about everything from pets to politics, but there was a strong undercurrent of mutual respect, accented with intelligence.

The "Real" stayed in *The Real World* for a couple more seasons—Pedro Zamora's presence in the San Francisco house being a highlight—but the slide into sluttiness, once it began, was unstoppable. Soon cast members were being chosen for their cup size, not their IQs. Drunken hot tub trysts became de rigueur, and cast members not only didn't care about politics, they probably couldn't spell it.

1973's *An American Family* got there first, but *The Real World* is credited for the modern resurgence of reality TV that brought us such treasures as *Jersey Shore* and *16 and Pregnant* and pretty much erased music videos from MTV. From real to unreal to crazy-wackadoodle surreal in just two decades.

STATUS: Still on MTV.

FUN FACT: You can live like a Real Worlder by renting the three-thousand-foot Palms Casino suite that was home to the 2002 Las Vegas cast—if you have fifteen thousand for one night, that is.

The Return of Donny Osmond

He may have claimed to be a little bit rock-and-roll, but audiences just weren't buying it. Seventies icon Donny Osmond—all gleaming choppers and eye-rolling corny jokes—found himself stuck in a career-endangering prison built by his own teenage success as a goody-two-shoes. Turns out, '80s audiences weren't exactly looking for middle-aged crooners who got their start on *The Andy Williams Show*.

That all changed in 1990, when he was cast in the hit stage musical *Joseph and the Amazing Technicolor Dreamcoat*. Suddenly, '90s kids fell in love with the talented, good-natured, and slightly goofy guy just like their moms did two decades earlier. Donnymania was everywhere. Audiences ate up his nice-guy appeal, first as the host of a popular syndicated TV talk show with his sister Marie, then as a voice in Disney's *Mulan*, and later when he took over Dick Clark's mic as host of *Pyramid*. He was back, baby, embracing his Donny destiny.

STATUS: Donny and Marie took their show to Vegas for a long-running cheese fest. In 2011, Donny showed off his fancy footwork and won the top prize on *Dancing with the Stars*.

FUN FACT: In 2006, Donny appeared in Weird Al Yankovic's "White & Nerdy" video.

Ring Pops

They were the only piece of bling that could give you type 2 diabetes. Ring Pops, the ubiquitous 1990s lollipops molded in the shape of a giant diamond, added a delicious new dimension to the world of candy jewelry. Kids who couldn't care less about cut, clarity, or carat weight were all about the most important "c" of all: corn syrup.

Like candy necklaces before them, Ring Pops were wearable snacks—both high fashion and high fructose. You could coordinate the color of the hundred-carat fruit-flavored gem to your outfit, and when you were looking for a sugar fix, the treat was just an arm's-length away. Some kids simply refused to take them off altogether, and accumulated everything from cat hair to pocket fuzz on the sticky surface. A quick dip in the drinking fountain, though, and they were good to go.

The popularity of Ring Pops prompted a rash of playground weddings. And why not? The little suckers were sweet, they were sparkly—and they didn't cost two months' salary. But then came the inevitable playground break-ups. Soon the merry-go-round was packed with six-year-old recent divorcées, all looking for a new sugar daddy.

STATUS: Bazooka—a division of Topps—still makes the little suckers, including a sugar-free version.

FUN FACT: There's even a brand of candy rings that light up.

Riot Grrrl

The '90s are famous for their boy bands, cute and nonthreatening as litters of puppies. But it was a musical movement run by the girls of the decade that smashed down gender barriers, capturing a young feminist sensibility and Do-It-Yourself mantra that still reverberates today.

On its surface, riot grrrl describes the group of mostly female '90s punk bands coming out of Washington, DC, and the Pacific Northwest with a musical mission. The songs of Bratmobile, Bikini Kill, and others were impassioned and angry, and they sang about real issues that affected the lives of young women without pulling punches or softening edges. More than that, they proved to a world used to seeing male lead singers and hearing the lyrics of male songwriters that the perspective of half the population deserved to take center stage too.

But the bands were only the most visible part of the scene. Girls inspired by the empowerment of the movement started zines, spoke out for political causes, gathered other girls and encouraged and taught them to do the same. Even a mainstream magazine, Jane Pratt's *Sassy*, spread the riot grrrl word. This generation of girls didn't believe for a minute that they couldn't do everything their brothers could, and then some. It was time for a revolution—grrrl style.

STATUS: Though many of the bands that sparked the riot grrrl movement are no more, the women who ran them hold diverse and often prominent roles in today's culture. Carrie Brownstein of pioneering riot grrrl band Sleater-Kinney co-created and stars in the TV series *Portlandia*.

FUN FACT: In 2011, NYU opened its Riot Grrrl Collection to scholars and researchers, featuring zines, artwork, journals, photographs, and more.

Rise of the Disney Princess

Like the British royal family, Disney's line of princesses had started to get a little musty and boring. Cinderella, Snow White, Sleeping Beauty—they were as familiar and yawn-inducing as Prince Charles's comb-over. But then, in the late 1980s and 1990s, a princess renaissance!

Ariel of *The Little Mermaid* swam into our hearts in 1989, and was quickly followed by Belle from *Beauty and the Beast*, Jasmine from *Aladdin*, Pocahontas, and Mulan. These were new-generation princesses. They loved their men, but they weren't passive slipper-losing, poisoned-apple-chomping, someday-my-prince-will-comers—Mulan, for one, pretty much singlehandedly saved China.

Not that the new-look princesses weren't a little loopy—Ariel hoarded trash, after all. But if you were a girl of trick-or-treating age in the 1990s, we'll bet you a pumpkin full of fun-size Snickers that you dressed as one of them for Halloween.

STATUS: Princesses of the 2000s include Tiana of *The Princess and the Frog*, Rapunzel of *Tangled*, and Merida of *Brave*.

FUN FACT: Belle and the Beast's final dance was done with reused animation from *Sleeping Beauty*.

Riverdance

Faith and begorra: If your parents forced you into taking Irish dance lessons—even though your last name is Martinez—you've likely got *Riverdance* to blame. The Irish stage show reeled and tapped its way to America in 1994, and taught us that Celtic culture had a lot more to offer than just Guinness and pots o' gold.

With arms at their sides and legs kicking and flicking like epileptic leprechauns, the dancers in *Riverdance*—including lead hoofer and choreographer Michael Flatley—sparked a resurgence of interest in all things Irish, even by people who assumed everybody on the Emerald Isle only ate yellow moons, pink hearts, and green clovers. Twenty-two million people in forty countries saw *Riverdance* live, and most left the theater doing a little jig.

STATUS: *Riverdance* mounted a farewell tour in 2012, and Flatley went on to lead other Irish dance shows like *Lord of the Dance* and *Feet of Flames*.

FUN FACT: In a 1998 episode of *Friends*, Chandler admits that Michael Flatley "scares the bejesus" out of him. ("His legs flail about as if independent from his body!")

Roller Shoes

While kids in the '80s vainly wished for a jet pack they could use to rocket around the playground, '90s kids actually got something almost as cool: roller shoes. Part Nike, part inline skate, roller shoes let kids wheel it up just by shifting their weight to their heels. Off they'd shoot, like prepubescent pool balls. Boys and girls who successfully begged their parents for a pair felt far superior to their classmates with more pedestrian footwear, and for good reason: Their feet were Transformers.

While most kids used them to roll from English class to Math, or from Cinnabon to Benetton, others took unexpected side trips into traffic or, we're assuming, down the occasional escalator. Some shoe-skaters took to the wheels like mini Wayne Gretzkys; others constantly careened out of control, banking into lockers and rolling into lakes. A growing pile of injuries prompted schools, malls, and even some towns—especially hilly ones—to ban the flying footwear. And God help the kid whose shoelaces came untied midroll and got tangled around the spinning wheel like spaghetti around a fork. Chin and teeth, meet sidewalk. Still, his likely last words before the doctors wired shut his jaw? "At least I didn't have to walk to the bus stop like the rest of you schmucks."

STATUS: Still zipping along. There's also a brand of footwear dubbed "spin shoes" that allow wearers to pirouette like a prima ballerina.

FUN FACT: On *Grey's Anatomy*, Dr. Arizona Robbins rolled around the hospital in a pair of roller shoes. Yep, they make adult-sized versions too.

Roseanne

They weren't the Huxtables, that's for sure. Unlike *The Cosby Show*'s lawyer and doctor couple, Roseanne and Dan Conner struggled to get by with menial jobs that rarely lasted. No New York nightlife or Malibu beach parties here—instead they bowled, wore sweatshirts, and lived in a small Illinois town. But the Conners' love for each other and their children wrapped the show like the grandma-style afghan that permanently draped their plaid couch.

Weight problems, elaborate Halloweens, and all, Dan and Roseanne were about the most relatable couple on TV in the '90s, and it was hard not to envy the smart, hilarious way they faced life head-on. "What did I tell you about killing your brother in the living room?" Roseanne chides Darlene in one scene. Dan and Roseanne weren't bitter about their working-class lives, but they wanted better for their kids. They taught them to bloom where they were planted, but also to dream big.

After eight rollicking seasons, the show pulled a fast one on viewers. The family supposedly won $108 million in the lottery—except in the final episode, Roseanne revealed the riches were just a dream brought on by her sorrow at Dan's early death from a heart attack. Even *M*A*S*H* didn't take its humor from such soaring heights to such utter sorrow this quickly. As in real life, the tears and the laughs were inseparable.

STATUS: *Roseanne* ended in 1997. In 2012, John Goodman signed on to costar with his former TV wife in a new NBC sitcom, *Downwardly Mobile*, but sadly for fans longing for a Conner couple reunion, the pilot was shelved.

FUN FACT: John Goodman's favorite vegetable, corn, is reportedly mentioned in every episode of the first season.

Salute Your Shorts

There are mullets, and then there's the coonskin-cap-meets-Garfield-pelt that sat on top of Danny Cooksey's head on *Salute Your Shorts*, which ran on Nickelodeon from 1991 to 1992. Before *Shorts*, Cooksey was best known for playing Sam, the little bowl-haircutted add-on in the final seasons of *Diff'rent Strokes*. But as troublemaker Bobby Budnick on *Salute Your Shorts*, Cooksey took his hair to a whole other place: Camp Anawanna. The catchy theme song said it all: "Camp Anawanna, we hold you in our hearts. And when we think about you, it makes me wanna fart!" Yep—for real. Stay classy, Nickelodeon.

Thanks to Budnick and fellow campers Sponge, Z.Z., Donkeylips, Dina, Telly, and the rest, every viewer wanted to pack up and head off to sleepaway camp. Even though camp life on the show was mostly shenanigans like putting somebody's boxer shorts up a flagpole, subjecting a kid to the dreaded Awful Waffle (pouring syrup on their stomach—don't ask), or having to look at Cooksey's hair. Good times, good times.

Those of us who later went on to real camps were upset to learn that they were heavy on macaroni crafts and canoeing and light on the syrup pranks and food fights that *Shorts* conditioned us to expect. Thankfully, though, Budnick was nowhere to be found.

STATUS: Nickelodeon aired reruns of the show as part of its The '90s Are All That late-night block in 2012.

FUN FACT: Cooksey went on to voice characters in animated shows like *G.I. Joe: Renegades*, *Pound Puppies*, and *Kung Fu Panda: Legends of Awesomeness*.

Saved by the Bell

Like a terribly written car accident, we just couldn't look away from *Saved by the Bell*, the best worst show of the 1990s. Every Saturday morning, we tuned in to watch preppy schemer Zack, nerd Screech, fashion-plate Lisa, cheerleader Kelly, preening jock Slater, and smart girl Jessie wrestle with issues like bullying, environmentalism, and addiction. The episode where Jessie lost it after getting hopped up on goofballs set a new standard for overacting—there are no words to describe the way she thrashed around, tearfully singing "I'm So Excited"—until Elizabeth Berkley beat her own record in *Showgirls*.

The show was as formulaic as it gets: Lisa would always rebuff Screech's sexually harassing advances, Zack would figure out some way to skate through class, and Slater would show up in a sleeveless T-shirt and mullet. What did we learn? Not much, other than Screech probably should have been in special ed, and Mr. Belding should have won the award for the most ineffectual principal in history, getting outfoxed almost every week by a group of fourteen-year-olds. (How many times can a guy fall for Zack pretending to be someone else on the phone? Answer: All of the times.)

It was cringe-inducing, but kids tuned in by the millions to watch the familiar group. *Bell* was a TV version of a bowl of Cap'n Crunch: sugary, comforting, and too much of it made your stomach hurt.

STATUS: In 1993, the show graduated into two spin-offs: *Saved by the Bell: The College Years* lasted for a season in primetime and wrapped up in a TV movie where Zack and Kelly got married in Las Vegas. *Saved by the Bell: The New Class* ran for seven seasons on Saturday mornings, and starred Mr. Belding—and nobody else you've ever heard of.

FUN FACT: *Saved by the Bell* started life as a different Saturday-morning show called *Good Morning, Miss Bliss*, and starred *The Parent Trap*'s Haley Mills. Zack, Lisa, Screech, and Mr. Belding were the only characters to make it to *SBTB*.

Scream

Jason Voorhees, Michael Myers, and Freddy Krueger ruled the '80s, but who would have guessed that ladies from *Party of Five* and *Friends* would be the ones to revitalize the horror genre in the '90s? Created by thrill-meister Wes Craven and *Dawson's Creek* auteur Kevin Williamson, *Scream* caught on with '90s audiences with its winky take on horror-movie clichés of decades past. The joke was that the kids in the movie knew everything there was to know about how to survive a horror movie (Never investigate scary noises or say, "I'll be right back."), but they were murdered anyway.

The twisty plot, dude-that's-so-meta approach, and legitimately freaky scares were what propelled *Scream* to become the highest-grossing slasher flick ever. And the cast didn't hurt either: It starred mega-wattage stars Neve Campbell and Courteney Cox, and dimmer bulbs like David Arquette and Jamie Kennedy.

Scream sliced into horror flicks with a self-referential knife—and gave new life to a genre that was very nearly six feet under.

"Do you like scary movies?" serial killer Ghostface would ask his victim before he drew blood. We sure did now.

STATUS: The original spawned—so far—three sequels. They've collectively earned more than $600 million at the box office. And in 2012, MTV announced plans to turn the movies into a TV show.

FUN FACT: At the last minute, a certain California school refused to allow the filmmakers to shoot there, and thus the closing credits offer "No thanks whatsoever to the Santa Rosa City School District Governing Board."

Scrunchies and Little Kid Barrettes

What Duchess of York Sarah Ferguson did for hair bows in the 1980s, Kelly Kapowski did for scrunchies in the '90s. And once the *Saved by the Bell* hottie wore them, '90s girls fell in love, and in line. Bye-bye, boring rubber bands that yanked on your hair like a crabby little sister. Hello, soft, fuzzy, fabric-covered piece of hairdo heaven. Crocheted scrunchies, denim scrunchies, scrunchies to match your cheerleading colors, satin scrunchies—there was one for every mood and outfit. Those whose hair wasn't long enough to scrunch got in on the trend by wearing them as bracelets.

At about the same time, Kelly Kapowski's fashion opposite, Courtney Love of Hole, popularized her own hair accessory. When Courtney started wearing little-kid barrettes snapped randomly through her hair, girls who longed to show that they were marching to their own drummer snapped back. The barrettes were cheap and easy to find, and it really didn't matter that they couldn't hold more than two or three hairs. Having a pastel pink airplane flying through your bangs or a light blue butterfly fluttering through your curls was more about the presentation, not the practicality.

If there was a message in 1990s hair accessories, it was simple: Do your own thing. Whether you wanted a subtle scrunchie to sweep your tresses off your neck or a plastic plaything to make a statement, there was no need to look like everyone else. Until 1994, when the Rachel came out.

STATUS: Still popular. If you're an Olympic gymnast (scrunchies) or a preschooler (barrettes).

Seinfeld

In the 1970s, Mary Tyler Moore made a family out of her coworkers, and in the 1980s, Sam Malone created one out of a bunch of barflies. In the 1990s, the most-loved family on TV consisted of Jerry, Elaine, George, and Kramer, four friends who would sell each other out in a New York minute for a prime parking spot and a marble rye.

Viewers may long to be as suave as cereal-eating, Superman-loving Jerry, but secretly we all kinda resembled George Costanza, wannabe marine biologist, near-professional parallel parker, and celebrator of Festivus. Crazy Kramer's schemes included trading Cuban cigars for golf, making salad in his shower, and letting Japanese businessmen sleep in his bureau. Elaine was the only woman to infiltrate the friend group, and she did it with style, except for when she was performing her weird little thumbs-up kicky dance.

But whereas *Mary Tyler Moore* ended with the entire cast in a group hug, *Seinfeld* would never go out on such a sentimental note. In the controversial last episode, the group ends up in jail for not stopping a carjacking, and more than a dozen minor characters return to testify against them. The show about nothing ended with its stars in jail—for doing nothing.

STATUS: It's only around in reruns and on DVDs. Not that there's anything wrong with that. Seinfeld cocreator Larry David's *Curb Your Enthusiasm* has similar sensibilities.

FUN FACT: The restaurant whose exterior was shown as Monk's Café, really Tom's Restaurant, was also the setting for Suzanne Vega's 1987 song, "Tom's Diner."

Skip-It

What's more fun than attaching a ball-and-chain to your ankle and swinging it around? Well, lots of things. But for some reason, Skip-It, the plastic version of the restraining device used on prisoners, had '90s girls thinking about committing grand larceny just so they could get sentenced to this brightly colored chain gang.

Once you'd mastered earlier jumping games such as hopscotch, this was apparently the next logical step. Skip-It looked like the float ball that sits in a toilet tank, only covered in charms and stickers and attached to a plastic leash. Kids would stick their ankle through the leash's hoop and start to skip, swinging the heavy plastic ball around like a multi-colored mace from Roman warrior days. Sure, sometimes it would connect with your ankle or another girl's knee. But whoever said life on the playground was all ponies and glitter?

Seventies girls had a simpler version of the toy, called Lemon Twist. Skip-It was a giant, uh, leap forward from its fruit-shaped forebear: Though it was introduced in the '80s, in the early '90s manufacturer Tiger Electronics added an ingenious element that only upped its addictive properties: an odometer. Yes, the new and improved toy now had a counter to track the number of successful swings you completed. It wasn't just play anymore; now Skip-It was a challenge. Girls would skip until after the sun went down, working their exhausted ankles to the bone to spin the thing around 999 times. And then they'd wake up the next morning and do it all over again.

A toy based on a staple of the penal system has never been so much fun.

STATUS: The original Skip-It died out in the late 2000s, but you can find knockoffs at toy stores and online.

FUN FACT: In 2011, *Time* magazine named Skip-It to its list of the one hundred greatest toys of all time.

Slap Bracelets

Kids always gravitate toward toys that possess that extra edge of danger. Cracking your head open on a Slip 'n Slide, impaling your friend with a lawn dart—that's as much a part of growing up as PB and Js. Slap bracelets translated that perilous play into jewelry form.

Less bracelets than toys, they were thin, fabric-covered ribbons of steel that would curl around one's wrist when cracked across

your arm. Some schools actually banned them, reportedly because the knockoff versions could wear down and cut a kid's arm, but we always suspected that the distraction factor was really what brought down the ban. At their peak, every kid in school was slapping them on and off during especially dull lectures or study hall.

Decked out with smiley faces, Bart Simpson, or tiger prints, none of them were too attractive, but beauty wasn't the point. It was all about the application—whacking your own limbs, or a friend's, then marveling as the bracelet grabbed an arm like Doc Octopus wrapping a tentacle around Spider-Man. They didn't hurt, but they really looked like they did. Joked comic Michael Ian Black, "It's for pre-teens who are into pre-bondage."

STATUS: In addition to the bracelets, there are now slap watches.

FUN FACT: Slap bracelets were invented by Stuart Anders, a Wisconsin shop teacher who was experimenting with thin bands of metal.

Snapple

Snapple drinks did for the 1990s what wine coolers did in the 1980s—invented an entirely new kind of beverage. Suddenly, everyone was toting the chubby glass bottles filled with a sweet blend of tea or fruit juice.

To look sharp, you popped your Snapple before twisting off the lid by smacking it on the flat of your palm several times, the kid version of tapping a pack of cigarettes before opening it. Underneath the cap, you found a random factoid, some of which were cool ("No piece of paper can be folded more than seven times") and some of which were just crazy ("Alaska has more caribou than people").

But maybe the coolest thing about Snapple was its ads, featuring the nasally New York–ish tones of Wendy Kaufman, a real employee who became known as the Snapple Lady and who answered reader mail. She gave the beverage its ideal image—a regular American, neither snootily pounding Perrier with the elite, nor downing Cokes with the herd.

The ads also claimed that Snapple was "made from the best stuff on earth." Which was . . . what, exactly? Unicorn tears? Calorie-free chocolate? Gold bullion? Our definitions of "best stuff" varied, but darned if we didn't drink it anyway.

STATUS: Available in grocery and convenience stores everywhere.

FUN FACT: Snapple Lady Wendy Kaufman reportedly started answering letters from Snapple lovers because she remembered how sad she was as a kid when Barry "Greg Brady" Williams didn't answer her fan letter.

Socker Boppers

S o let us get this straight: Socker Boppers were blow-up boxing gloves that let kids beat the living snot out of each other, and our parents didn't mind? Yup. We can't really fault Mom and Dad, though, since the toys looked harmless enough—and every kid in the commercial was smiling, even though we're pretty sure we saw a few teeth and a little trickle of blood flying out of one boy's mouth.

Kids everywhere blew into the giant, inflatable fists until they were light-headed—bordering on fainting—and then stepped into the ring. Ding, ding! We'd pretend to be Mike Tyson (except we rarely bit each other's ears off), jabbing, poking, and uppercutting each other with inflatable impunity. Even though the fists of balloon-y death were cushioned, a direct hit stung like a dodgeball to the face. Or they'd suddenly pop, and you'd find yourself get-

ting pummeled with bare knuckles. You'd never catch a kid complaining, though. Because everybody knew that the first rule of Socker Boppers is you don't talk about Socker Boppers.

STATUS: You can still buy the originals, as well as Socker Bopper Swords.

FUN FACT: For a time, Socker Boppers changed its name to "Sock'em Boppers."

Sour Candy

In the 1990s, candy trends scoffed at sweet and dove into the super-sour, with everything from cute little Sour Patch Kids to long and lanky Sour Punch Straws to tongue-burning Warheads getting in on the game.

Super-sour candy allowed you to challenge your recess buddies to a duel for sucking supremacy. How long could you savor a pucker-producing Mega Warhead? Who could shove more of the tart tongue twisters in his mouth without spitting them back out? You'd fight to keep the candy inside by pretending you were James Bond being tortured by a megalomaniacal super-villain, and later create your own candy-centered gang initiation for the new kid in school.

Overdose on the sour stuff and you could actually injure the little bumps on your tongue, a reaction you'd feel for days afterward whenever you ate anything. But if you tricked yourself into sticking it out, most sour candy gave up the ghost almost immediately, turning into something as mild as a lemon drop in under a minute. Shockingly bold, then suddenly gentle as a grandpa, it was the Ozzy Osbourne of candy trends.

STATUS: Still making kids pucker.

FUN FACT: For a while, you could even buy Mega Warheads toothpaste. The tube encouraged users to "take the brushing challenge," warned that use would make your gums tingle, and also flat-out told you to also brush with a fluoride paste.

Spice Girls

In the 1990s, girls were everywhere, from the garage rock–blasting riot grrrl scene to the vampire-staking Buffy the Vampire Slayer. One of the splashiest manifestations of all that euphoric estrogen was Britain's Spice Girls, a female answer to the boy bands that were hogging radio airwaves.

Young fans told their parents what they wanted, what they really, really wanted, and it was Spice Girls everything, from dolls to lollipops to a Polaroid camera dubbed the Spice Cam. Every radio-listening girl of a certain age immediately chose a favorite—Sporty, Baby, Posh, Scary, or Ginger—much in the same way their

big sisters once identified with Kelly, Jill, or Sabrina on *Charlie's Angels*.

The group was as prefab as the Monkees or Menudo, but their sense of Girl Power felt real and joyous. Not all their lyrics made sense ("I wanna really, really, really wanna zig-a-zig ah"), but the soaring chorus of "Wannabe" pounded home the idea that friends topped flings and sisterhood was still powerful. "Make it last forever, friendship never ends," cooed the lyrics of that 1996 hit. It didn't, of course, as Geri "Ginger Spice" Halliwell left the band in 1998 and things fell apart from there, but stars like Britney Spears, Christina Aguilera, and Mandy Moore forever owe a debt of thanks to their swinging sisters from across the pond.

STATUS: The former Spice Girls float in and out of the spotlight (including a high-profile gig at the 2012 Summer Olympics), as do newer girl groups, including various incarnations of the Pussycat Dolls.

FUN FACT: Their 1997 movie, *Spice World*, scored at the box office but flopped with critics. Wrote Roger Ebert, "(The girls) occupy *Spice World* as if they were watching it."

Spuds Mackenzie

Look up "It's a dog's life" in the dictionary, and you'll find a picture of Spuds MacKenzie, the luckiest bull terrier in the world. Once Bud Light anointed the furry little guy its beer mascot in 1987, Spuds traded in his leash and rabies tags for a tuxedo and cool shades. Through the early '90s, Spuds had women fawning over him, frat boys pampering him, and got invited to all the best keggers. Not a bad gig for a pup who looked like Petey from the Little Rascals, but drunk.

With his stout and wrinkly Ernest Borgnine looks, Spuds had an every-dog appeal. He was kind of like your college roommate: He lazed around all the time, rarely wore pants, and probably farted constantly. And we loved him for it, gobbling up his posters and stuffed animals by the millions. So much, in fact, that Anheuser-Busch faced accusations that it was using the party animal to market beer to kids.

Spuds died in 1993 of kidney failure, which was a surprise because after his years as a party animal, we were expecting something to do with the liver. But before he went to that great keg-filled kennel in the sky, he came clean: Turns out he wasn't a "he" at all—it was revealed that Spuds was actually a girl, and named Honey Tree Evil Eye.

STATUS: Spuds has been replaced by other animal mascots, including those damn singing frogs: "Bud. Weis. Er."

FUN FACT: Spuds McKenzie was name-checked in Tone Loc's hit single, "Funky Cold Medina."

Squeezit Drinks

When you reached an age when you would rather be seen drinking from a baby bottle than a juice box, you knew you'd graduated to Squeezits. The colorful drinks came in tall, cartoon-shaped bottles that you'd squirt into your mouth with all the passion of Lance Armstrong grabbing a water break during the Alps stage of the Tour de France. You'd beg mom to stow them in your lunch in place of milk, feeling so superior to your pals stuck with Hi-C or Capri Sun.

Like Funny Face drinks before them, Squeezit flavors had their own names and personalities, from Berry B. Wild to Smarty Arty Orange. Which was both cool and disturbing, especially thanks to a commercial that showed kids grabbing Squeezits from the fridge and squishing them torturously as the cartoon bottles cringed and tried to hide in the Jell-O. But the best part was how the drinks eschewed straws or sipping, encouraging kids to just squeeze the sticky juice straight into their mouths. We didn't know it then, but it was great training for college days of beer bongs and chug-a-lugs.

STATUS: Squeezits were squeezed out around 2001. Kool-Aid Bursts are similar, but true Squeezit fans remain unsatisfied.

FUN FACT: For a brief time, one Squeezit version came with tablets that you would drop in to change the juice's color.

Star Trek: The Next Generation

So you say you never got into *Star Trek: The Next Generation?* Watch a few reruns. You will be assimilated.

Not all Trek fans were on board in 1987 when the series first dared to boldly go where a horny Captain Kirk and logical Mr. Spock had gone before. But somehow the new version blasted through the old show's cheesy outdated elements like a phaser through a loaf of Velveeta.

Captain Jean-Luc Picard made baldness sexy, and he was never led around by his Little Trouser Captain in quite the way Kirk was. Tough-talking Lieutenant Worf reminded us that the Klingons were the galaxy's true badasses—complete with a death ritual where survivors let out a bloodcurdling scream to warn the dead that a Klingon warrior was coming. And in *ST: TNG*, women didn't just wear short skirts and flirt with Kirk—they were medical officers, security, engineers, and more, ranking right up there with the men.

The world of *Next Generation* was a sort of idealized version of our own, the fair and just future we all hoped we'd warp into someday. Space could be terrifying (those Borg!) but back on the Enterprise, Captain Picard was always calm, the final frontier always tantalizingly waiting just out of reach, a juicy reward for those brave enough to go sailing through the stars.

STATUS: *Star Trek: TNG* ended in 1994, but creator Gene Roddenberry's concept continues to live on, with *Star Trek* movies rebooting the original series.

FUN FACT: According to the *Star Trek: The Next Generation Companion* book, young crew member Wesley Crusher was originally supposed to be a girl, Leslie Crusher.

Star Wars Prequel Mania

In 1999, sixteen years since the final Ewok was dry-cleaned and put away, George Lucas finally went back to the intergalactic drawing board. When the news hit that the bearded Jedi master was readying a new *Star Wars* flick, *Star Wars: Episode I—The Phantom Menace*, a generation was as thrilled as Jabba the Hutt at an all-you-can-eat buffet. Expectations were higher than Princess Leia on the *Star Wars Holiday Special*.

Sadly, what showed up on-screen was . . . a steaming pile of Jar

Jar. It was all wooden acting and a pre-Vader Anakin Skywalker running around in space-Pampers, combined with super-exciting political intrigue like the Imperial Senate worrying about a trade disputezzzz—sorry. Fell asleep there for a minute.

The Force wasn't exactly with this film—or the next one, or the next—but that didn't stop nerds from lining up for weeks and paying Super Bowl prices for first-night tickets. The original three movies had come out a long time ago, in a decade far, far away, and a new generation of Jedi had been born in a world that had never not known *Star Wars*. These weren't the droids we were looking for, but we didn't know that going in.

STATUS: The force is still with *Star Wars*, with video games, the *Clone Wars* TV series, and 3-D versions of the prequels. In 2012, Lucas sold out to Disney, which promptly announced plans for a new trilogy of *Star Wars* movies.

FUN FACT: Jake Lloyd, who played little Anakin, said that his childhood was turned into a "living hell" because other children would make lightsaber noises whenever they saw him.

Surge Soda

If an asteroid ever crashed into the woods behind your house and dripped a strange glowing fluid that turned all your farm animals into vampiric cannibals, yeah, it'd probably look a lot like Surge soda. Was it green? Was it yellow? Surge was a mix of the

two, maybe the color you'd get if you soaked a highlighter in a glass full of lime Jell-O.

Coke brought Surge to the U.S. in 1997, supposedly as a competitor for Pepsi's Mountain Dew. Citrusy and tangy, the mega-caffeinated drink was a hit with kids, but sales quickly fell off. Ads tried to push it as an extreme-sports beverage, a kind of pre–Red Bull energy drink. But the Surge slowed to a trickle and in the early 2000s vanished from store shelves.

In one of the 1990s' weirdest commercials, urban kids line up a bunch of couches in the street, then leap over them to get to a bottle of Surge. If you sensibly asked why they didn't just run around the couches, you were obviously not Surge's target market.

STATUS: Long gone—in the U.S., that is. You can still buy Surge in Norway, where it's called Urge.

FUN FACT: Two 1990s icons met when Surge made an appearance on *Buffy the Vampire Slayer*.

Swing Dancing

While kids of the '90s were jumpin', jivin', and wailin' like swing dancing was their very own invention, their grandparents were shaking their heads and cautioning the whippersnappers to take care of their hips. Been there, danced that.

Still, the craze was new to us, and swept across the decade like a zoot-suited tidal wave, resurrected from the '30s and '40s by modern groups with names like drinks (Squirrel Nut Zippers! Cherry Poppin' Daddies!). The 1998 Gap commercial featuring ultra-enthusiastic khaki-clad dancers flipping each other around to Louis Prima's "Jump, Jive an' Wail" was hugely responsible (or to blame, depending on your point of view) for the revival. The other culprit? *Swingers*, the 1996 flick that celebrated the loungy, cocktail-fueled lifestyle of Vince Vaughn and Jon Favreau, whose metabolisms at the time allowed them to eat whatever they wanted without fear of getting doughy.

They were so money, and they didn't even know it. And so was swing dancing—until it faded away again into just another wing-tipped, Lindy-Hopped, wide-tied memory. It's scheduled for another return in 2052.

STATUS: Faded back into yesteryear, until our grandkids inevitably pick it back up.

FUN FACT: In 1994, ten-year-old Benji Schwimmer taught Regis and Kathie Lee how to swing dance on their show. Twelve years later, Schwimmer went on to win *So You Think You Can Dance*.

TGIF and SNICK

Beginning in the 1980s, television networks started to attach nicknames to especially powerful parts of their schedule. NBC made the biggest splash with its Thursday-night Must-See TV, but it was Nickelodeon's SNICK and ABC's TGIF that are remembered most fondly by children of the 1990s.

SNICK stood for "Saturday Night Nickelodeon," and for kids too young to go out on dates but too old to go to bed early, it was a slice of basic-cable heaven. SNICK offerings included such treats as *Ren and Stimpy*, *Clarissa Explains It All*, *All That*, *Rugrats*, and more. The block even had a mascot—the big orange couch.

Everyone knew TGIF as short for "Thank God It's Friday," but ABC claimed that the initials for its Friday-night programming stood for "Thank Goodness It's Funny." And it usually was, with shows like *Family Matters*, *Step by Step*, and *Boy Meets World* starting off your weekend with laughs.

But on TV, nothing's funny forever. As the shows declined in popularity, and the age group raised on them started to drive and go out on weekends, the programming blocks fell away. But everything old is new again. Nickelodeon started highlighting its old 1990s shows again in 2011 under the name The '90s Are All That. They really were, weren't they?

STATUS: Friday and Saturday nights are now sad dead zones where little-loved TV shows go to die.

Taco Bell Chihuahua

Why did we ever let a dog advise us on fast-food choices? Dogs are hardly connoisseurs of Mexican cuisine. Dogs will eat their own vomit. But in the 1990s, Gidget the Taco Bell Chihuahua sashayed her way to commercial stardom.

The wide-eyed little purse dog was female, yet it was supposed to represent the chain's prime customer, a smart-alecky, sometimes bratty teen male. In true teenage boy form, it tried to trap Godzilla, mimicked Che Guevara, and broke into people's apartments, all in search of its spicy quick fix.

Most notably, of course, it never failed to deliver the accented slogan, "*Yo quiero* Taco Bell." If you watched TV in the 1990s, this may have been the only Spanish you knew.

STATUS: Taco Bell stopped the ad campaign in 2001. Gidget died in 2009. The fast-food chain has moved on to many different ad campaigns, and one even featured another animal mascot—Snowball, a dancing cockatoo.

FUN FACT: On a 1998 episode of *The Tonight Show*, Jay Leno joked that the dog's final words would be, "I'm going to see what they do in the kitchen."

Talk Show Boom

In the '90s, talk show hosts multiplied like trash-TV Gremlins. Ricki Lake, Cosby Kid Tempestt Bledsoe, Donny and Marie, Mark Walberg (not that one, the other one), Jenny Jones, Montel Williams, Sally Jesse Raphael, Carnie Wilson, Geraldo, fitness guru Susan Powter, and even former *90210*-er Gabrielle Carteris all had daytime gigs. If you wanted to see a double amputee who married a horse and now wanted to find his birth mother, your odds were pretty good you'd find that combination on at least one of the shows.

What was it about the 1990s that turned the TV talk genre into a total free-for-all? Promises of big syndication money, for one. And as more and more folks signed up for satellite and cable, all the new channels had to fill their programming space with something. And often, especially when it came to daytime, something weird.

Mornings and afternoons may have been crowded, but late-night hosts popped up like pimples too. Pat Sajak, Keenen Ivory Wayans, Dennis Miller, and Lauren Hutton all hosted after-dark talkfests. Remember Magic Johnson's short-lived show? We use every fiber of our being trying not to, and still get uncomfortable thinking about it.

But when it comes to talk-show flops, Fox's *The Chevy Chase Show* took the biggest pratfall of all. *Time* magazine summed it up by saying that the visibly nervous host "brought too little experience and too much ego" to the show and that his comic sensibility was "too dated." Ouch. The program lasted for five weeks in 1993, barely long enough for the paint to dry on the host's parking space, but the jokes about it will go on forever.

STATUS: The '90s talk show boom faded almost as quickly as it arrived, although celebrities still occasionally poke their well-manicured toes in the talk-show waters (ahem, Tony Danza).

FUN FACT: The TV Guide Network named *The Chevy Chase Show* to its list of the "Twenty-five Biggest TV Blunders."

Tamagotchi

Remember that assignment you got in fifth grade, where you had to treat a raw egg as if it were your own child? That was the idea behind Tamagotchi, the huge 1990s fad which provided a digital version of the egg project—only this time, you didn't need to worry about your mom accidentally making it into an omelet.

You were obligated to feed, clean up after, and even play with your little creature, or it would eventually breathe its last digital breath. Three buttons let you play God—and forced you to constantly run back to your locker to give it a snack, pick up its poop, or give it some exercise. Most annoying was the constant beeping and booping, like it was a starving Coleco Electronic Football game. Some schools banned the needy little things, and more than one parent probably stumbled into their kids' rooms in the middle of the night and smashed it with a hammer because it just wouldn't stop peeping.

Still, the virtual creature in a key fob was the perfect starter pet, because if your Tamagotchi died, all you needed to do was reset it—unlike when a real pet died and you had to give it a burial at sea via the toilet.

STATUS: They're still around. Now Tamagotchis have an online element and, most important, a way to turn off the sound.

FUN FACT: The virtual pet sparked its own psychological term: The Tamagotchi Effect supposedly describes when a human develops an emotional attachment to a machine.

Tan M&M's

First off, who was choosing colors for M&M's candies anyway? They had the entire rainbow at their service, and yet they picked not one, but two shades of brown. Did those same

folks also feel that buttons were too daring a form of clothing fastener, and that milk should be replaced with a tamer beverage, like water?

Whether you called it light brown, tan, or "that color all M&M's turn once they get a little sweaty in your pocket," tan M&M's were few people's favorite and always an also-ran to big brother dark brown.

So in 1995, Mars decided to stop tanning for good, holding a nationwide contest to replace the color. Ten million candy lovers called 1-800-FUN-COLOR to vote for either pink, purple, or blue. Blue washed away the competition with 54 percent of the vote, and the tan treats vanished. Never fear. You can still get them back if you just lick a handful of the dark brown or red ones for a while.

STATUS: While you can go to specialty candy stores and custom-select M&M's in shades ranging from aqua to electric green to gold, tan remains unavailable. It's the shunned taupe sheep of the family who's never invited home for the holidays.

Teddy Ruxpin

You know the audio-animatronic Abraham Lincoln at Walt Disney World's Hall of Presidents, with his metal skeleton and creepy robot eyes that have just a glint of life to them? He's a close cousin of Teddy Ruxpin. Although the bear robot was even freakier. Because when was the last time Abe Lincoln mauled you while you slept?

The battery-powered bear robot initially came to creepy life in 1985, moving its eyes and jaw in synch with the cassette tape in its backside. When its original manufacturer filed for Chapter 11 two years later, though, Teddy went into hibernation. In the '90s, Hasbro picked up the license—and invoked the technological black arts to raise the unholy bear from the dead. Now, instead of cassettes, it used higher-tech cartridges. But it still ran on batteries, and also, we're pretty sure, on children's night-mares.

Didn't humanity learn its lesson when it built Skynet and gave the machines self-awareness? With Teddy Ruxpin, society is just a microchip upgrade away from bear-shaped Terminators roaming the Earth, reading bedtime stories while they enslave us all.

STATUS: While several companies tried to spark a Teddy comeback, they were off store shelves by 2010. But we don't think we've seen the last of Teddy: Just like the Terminator, he'll be back.

FUN FACT: As a kid during show-and-tell, future Black Eyed Peas frontman Will.i.am used his sister's Teddy Ruxpin to play the songs he'd written and recorded.

Teenage Mutant Ninja Turtles

Somewhere deep underground, the Teenage Mutant Ninja Turtles must have had one heckuva marketing machine. For a certain age group of boys in the 1990s, if you didn't carry a Turtle lunchbox, sleep on Turtle bed linens, or at least have a fistful of the action figures stuffed in your cubby or locker, you might as well quit school and go live in the sewers yourself.

Heroes on the half-shell Leonardo, Michelangelo, Raphael,

and Donatello leapt from indie comic books to their own TV cartoon in the 1980s, and by the 1990s, their images—and their action figures—were everywhere. It wasn't hard to see why. They combined so many things that we loved, it was as if they were created by a group of kids who threw every awesome idea they could think of into a blender. They ate pizza! They fought crime with wicked weapons like staffs and nunchakus! They talked like surfers! They lived in the sewers! They reported to a mutant rat! Just like us—except our sewers were just messy bedrooms and our mutant rat was Miss Dedman, the math teacher.

Why did the Turtles bother to wear masks, anyway? Only those same nimrods who couldn't tell Clark Kent was Superman would be unable to figure out that the four gigantic, carb-loading, anthropomorphic green guys next door were probably the superheroes everybody kept talking about. Cowabunga, dude.

STATUS: It's turtle time once again. In 2012, they returned in a Nickelodeon series, and there's talk of a new big-screen version as early as 2014.

FUN FACT: In the 1990 live-action movie, villain Splinter was played by Kevin Clash, formerly the voice of Elmo.

Terrible *Saturday Night Live* Movies

The '90s were chock-full of *SNL* spin-off flicks, and only two—*Wayne's World* and *Wayne's World 2*—were better than horrible. *Coneheads*, *A Night at the Roxbury*, *Stuart Saves His Family*, and *Superstar* each have their moments, but mostly they smell like Lorne Michaels left a few million dollars' worth of raw shrimp out in the sun.

The worst offender, by every possible method of measurement, is *It's Pat*, the 1992 flop starring Julia Sweeney as the androgynous title character. The groan-worthy gender-confusion plot worked in tiny doses on TV, but when the very gross Pat, dressed in horn-rimmed glasses, a western shirt, and black, curly hair, made it to the big screen, America stayed home in droves. For some reason, people were unwilling to pay good money to sit in a theater and cringe as Pat made uncomfortable noises and wiped his or her hands on his or her shirt. The best thing about the film? It was only seventy-seven minutes long.

STATUS: They keep making 'em. *MacGruber*, anyone?

FUN FACT: *It's Pat* includes Aerosmith's classic song "Dude (Looks Like a Lady)."

"The More You Know" Public Service Announcements

Public-service announcements take many forms, from the fried egg of "this is your brain on drugs" to the druggie son-and-dad's "I learned it by watching you!" Starting in 1989, NBC cut right to the chase with its short-and-sweet "The More You Know" campaign. An actor, anchor, or other famous person pops up, delivers a few sentences about the cause du jour, and wham, bam, the star-comet logo soars across the screen and those four addictive notes pound out the theme.

George Clooney would rather you not hit your kids! Bill Cosby wonders if you've ever considered teaching! Betty White suggests that you read! David Schwimmer wants you to stop your friends from raping drunk girls! Kathy Griffin shadowboxes with a turtle! Not really sure what that last one was about.

Sometimes the star is so random you're not really sure who they are, except that they surely have a show on NBC. Sometimes the cause seems to have been chosen as a drunken challenge. (Ask your doctor about bone density? Plant trees to prevent asthma?) But the simplicity and shortness is hard to beat. If after-school specials had only thirty seconds and one chair for a prop, they'd be "The More You Know."

STATUS: NBC still cranks 'em out.

Thomas Kinkade Art

Move over, Currier and Ives. In the 1990s, Thomas Kinkade's snow-covered mansions, babbling brooks, and glowing churches replaced you as the sappiest art in the universe. Whether depicted on paintings, Christmas cards, tote bags, or night-lights, there is something unnervingly, Stepford-ly creepy about Kinkade's rainbow-skied universe.

In Kinkade's world, houses are "cottages," Christmas is "yuletide," and everyone has their own gazebo and/or lighthouse. Don't get us started on the random color choices. Why is that patch of snow glowing pink?

And ever notice how a Kinkade house features light blazing not from just one window, but from every single orifice? Either that place is on fire, or somewhere in there our dad is walking around lecturing about the electric bill and snapping switches off as fast as the artist can turn them on again.

STATUS: Still very popular, despite Kinkade's untimely death in 2012.

FUN FACT: Jared Padalecki of *Supernatural* fame plays Kinkade in the 2008 DVD movie *Thomas Kinkade's Christmas Cottage*, produced by Kinkade himself.

Tickle Me Elmo Craze

Ever see a stampede of buffalo? Now imagine them with credit cards, sharp elbows, and a laser focus on snagging a rare, goofy, giddy doll, and you're getting close to the frenzied pandemonium that overtook toy stores when Tickle Me Elmo came to town. The little red Muppet would chuckle when you pressed his belly, then started to freak out into a giggly frenzy the more you squeezed. (More than a few frazzled parents dreamed of squeezing and squeezing until Elmo suddenly stopped, but we digress.)

Sparked in part by Rosie O'Donnell featuring the laughing fuzz ball on her show, mobs of Muppet-lusting shoppers descended on unsuspecting stores in 1996. One unlucky Walmart clerk was trampled by the crowd and suffered a concussion, broken rib, and injuries to his knee, back, and jaw. ("Today's stampede was brought to you by the letter 'T,' for traction.")

Still, the fervor paid off for at least a few savvy shoppers. Some quick-on-the-draw buyers who snapped up the hysterical doll turned right around and scalped it for as much as fifteen hundred dollars. Who's laughing now, Elmo?

STATUS: In 2006, Playschool unveiled the Tickle Me Elmo X-treme (T.M.X.), which amped up Elmo's laughing to near psychotic levels. The little guy rolled around on the floor in histrionics, begging you to stop.

FUN FACT: On *The Simpsons*, Millhouse got a Tickle Me Krusty, which cackled lines like, "Hooo ha ha ha! Hey, kid, get your finger outta there."

Topsy Tail

Topsy Tail taught 1990s girls a valuable lesson that resonated well beyond the world of cheap hair products: As-seen-on-TV purchases never quite make the leap from TV to the real world.

On the ads, women waved a tiny plastic noose through their lush locks and seconds later were sporting an exotically complicated ponytail, braid, or updo. The commercial even promised you could Topsy Tail your thick tresses for your wedding.

But if you actually sent in your hard-earned cash and ordered the thing, were you ever in for a surprise. Turns out the tiny plastic noose doesn't actually come with its own stylists, and what took seconds in the ad took hours while you sweatily squinted at the instructions and tried desperately to recreate them in your own bathroom mirror.

You could only stab yourself in the neck a few times before giving up and tossing the Topsy Tail into the drawer next to the curling iron, the crimper, the foam curlers, the heated rollers, and three cans of long-expired mousse.

STATUS: You can still buy Topsy Tails, but the bouffanty Bump-It is a more recent take on mail-order DIY hair design.

FUN FACT: In 1994, Tyco made a doll dubbed My Pretty Topsy Tail, who came with floor-length hair and her own miniature Topsy Tail.

Troll Dolls

Has there ever been an uglier, weirder fad than troll dolls? They sport wildly colored hair, faces like unbaked pretzel dough, and clothes straight outta the *Brady Bunch*'s Goodwill donation pile. Yet somehow they just keep becoming popular. Nineties kids snapped up the so-ugly-they're-cute creatures by the outstretched armful just as their parents did in the 1960s. And here we thought insanity skipped a generation.

For girls, trolls offered a diverse doll universe minus Barbie's eating disorders and angst over Ken. In Troll Land, a shrimpy Santa troll might preside over the wedding of a giant pink-haired bride and green-haired groom dressed up as the Easter bunny. Nudist trolls with gems for bellybuttons drank tea with grandma trolls with rainbow hair, and nobody got judge-y or uptight.

Boys were a harder sell. Hasbro tried to suck them into the fad in 1992 with the release of the Original Battle Trolls, who were armed with weapons and painful, constipated-looking expressions even creepier than their traditional-troll counterparts. We can't imagine why Hasbro lost that war.

The one concession boys made to the trend: For some reason, troll pencil toppers were exceptionally popular with both genders. Although since the pencil pretty much impaled the troll's butt, they looked as if they were being tortured for witchcraft in seventeenth-century Salem.

STATUS: They're everywhere!

FUN FACT: Drew's arch-nemesis Mimi on *The Drew Carey Show* was obsessed with the creepy critters. In one episode, she tried to replace all of the store's mannequins with giant troll dolls.

Turbo Football

Many thanks, Nerf, for developing the foam-based technology that allowed even sports-averse nerds to throw a football with pinpoint accuracy. The Turbo was molded with grooves that made it easy to grip, and aerodynamic enough to let you throw a perfect spiral faster than Brett Favre could change his mind about retiring. Far better than a standard light and airy Nerf ball, the Turbo was heavier, denser, and harder, and cut through the air like a lawn dart.

The Turbo made a benchwarmer into a mini–Joe Montana. But, of course, when you tried out for the JV team with your new-found, Nerf-centered confidence, you got smacked in the face with reality—and by a seventh-grade tackler. Still, Nerf continued to make more and more elaborate versions, outfitted with bells and whistles, like the Screamer, which let out a high-pitched whine, and the Turbo Liquidator, which was wrapped with a "gyrowave" ring filled with liquid. The classic Turbo remained the most sought-after, though. We swear we chucked one into the air in 1992 and it still hasn't come down.

STATUS: Today, Nerf makes a Turbo Jr., but it doesn't have the same design as the '90s version.

FUN FACT: In 2004, one of the Turbo's descendants was pulled from store shelves for being too dangerous. Nerf's Big Play Football featured a flip-open top with an erasable writing pad inside to jot down plays. It was also a lot harder than your average Nerf ball. According to the Consumer Product Safety Commission, at least eight people had to get stitches after they got smacked in the face with it.

Upper Deck
Baseball Cards

Remember when collecting baseball cards was about the thrill of the hunt, and not whether your Ken Griffey Jr. rookie card was going to pay for your college education? That all changed in 1989 with the arrival of upstart trading-card company Upper Deck. Suddenly, even kids saw dollar signs and moved their collections from shoe boxes to safe-deposit boxes.

The company's novel gimmicks were as thrilling as an inside-the-park home run. Every card featured a shiny hologram, and real player autographs and jersey swatches were randomly inserted into some card boxes. (About as randomly as a Cubs win, as we didn't know anyone who actually ended up with a Reggie Jackson sweat-stained elbow piece.) Upper Deck jump-started the collector's market, and kids were convinced that someday they would trade in their piles of cards for a mansion and a yacht. Suddenly, it paid to keep cards in mint condition instead of clothes-pinning them to the spokes of your bike.

Upper Deck didn't even come with the slabs of powder-sprinkled gum other companies tucked in alongside Cal Ripken Jr. and Wade Boggs. Gum was for kids; this was serious business. According to the *New York Times*, in 1980, Topps and Fleer were kings of a $50-million industry. By 1992, with Upper Deck in the mix, sports cards had become a $1.5-billion juggernaut. But while the card companies made a bundle, few kids cleaned up. Alas, most of us had to rely on student loans to pay for college. Thanks for nothing, Ken Griffey Jr.

STATUS: Still going strong. Upper Deck eventually expanded into everything from golf to lacrosse to Hello Kitty cards.

FUN FACT: Upper Deck has even produced cards featuring actual autographs and—no lie—strands of real hair from historical figures like Babe Ruth, George Washington, and Abe Lincoln.

Urkel

Steve Urkel of *Family Matters* appears to have been created by a screenwriter who simply listed as many annoying traits as he could think of, then wrapped them all into one character. One whiny, clumsy, doltish character.

There's absolutely no explanation for Jaleel White's Urkel becoming a massive national hit, but it happened. What Fonzie and J. R. Ewing were to the 1970s and 1980s, the doofus-y little friend of the Winslow family was to the 1990s. Was the appeal his high-water pants and suspenders? His enormous glasses? That creepy dance? That voice, like a mouse on helium? His cloying catchphrases, like "Did I do that?"

Whatever it was, it worked. *Family Matters* ran for a whopping nine seasons.

Urkel also sold products. There were T-shirts, talking dolls, and an infamous short-lived strawberry-banana cereal called Urkel-Os. Like Urkel's popularity itself, the cereal probably seemed like a good idea at the time, but made less and less sense in the cold hard light of day.

STATUS: Urkel may be nothing but an annoying memory, but Sheldon Cooper of *The Big Bang Theory* shares Urkel's nerdiness and questionable fashion sense.

FUN FACT: Jaleel White auditioned for the role of Rudy on *The Cosby Show* back when the show had yet to decide if the Huxtables' youngest would be a girl or a boy.

Violent Video Games

Today's gamers mow down hundreds of photo-realistic enemy troops, zombies, and aliens before breakfast. But it wasn't always first-person hack-and-slash. In the '90s, geysers of pixelated blood washed over the video game industry for the very first time. The gratuitous carnage hit so quickly and so hard, it probably made happy-go-lucky Pac-Man barf up a few ghosts.

One of the first games to embrace uber-bloody gore was 1992's *Mortal Kombat*. Two warriors would punch and kick each other, until one could barely stand up. The winner would finish his opponent by pulling off his arms or yanking his head and spine out and holding it up like a trophy. (Way to promote nonviolent playground activity.) The next year saw the arrival of *Doom*, which added 3-D graphics and a first-person perspective to the macabre mix.

Gory as they were, these were the first really addicting games—digital meth. You'd flip them on and the next thing you knew, it was eight months later, you had a long beard and were surrounded by several jars of your own urine and messages telling you not to bother coming in to your job at Cinnabon.

STATUS: *Mortal Kombat* and *Doom* spawned several forgettable movies, and cleared a path for similar games like *Halo*, *Resident Evil*, and *Call of Duty*. *Grand Theft Auto* even allows players to murder police officers and prostitutes. *Q*bert*, it ain't.

FUN FACT: According to IMDb.com, in the *Mortal Kombat* movie, Tom Cruise and Johnny Depp were considered for the role of main fighter Johnny Cage, which eventually went to Linden Ashby. Who? Exactly.

Waterworld

With liquid everywhere, why the hell was everyone in *Waterworld* so filthy? The characters' inexplicable aversion to taking a quick dip in the ocean that surrounded them wasn't the only confusing thing about Kevin Costner's 1995 flick. For instance: If the budget was a ridiculous $175 million—at the time the most expensive film ever made—then why did child-star Tina Majorino's wig look like a rabid sea otter? And, who wanted to see Kevin Costner as a brooding post-apocalyptic fish man who drinks his own purified pee, anyway? Answer: Probably the same people who paid to see him as a brooding post-apocalyptic mailman in *The Postman* a few years later.

Critics dubbed the flick *Fishtar*, after the spectacular Warren Beatty/Dustin Hoffman 1987 mega-flop *Ishtar*. Audiences may have argued about just how much *Waterworld* stank like rotting fish, but everyone agreed on one thing: It was a very moist *Mad Max* rip-off, with jet skis instead of motorcycles and a gill-eared, web-toed Costner instead of Mel Gibson.

STATUS: 2012's *Battleship* was another waterlogged, big-budget flick. Kevin Costner even gave director Peter Berg advice on how to successfully shoot scenes on the ocean.

FUN FACT: In the opening credits, the globe in the Universal logo morphs into a world with the ice melted and the continents submerged. Some call this the best part of the entire film.

Wayne's World

Public-access shows started to explode in the 1990s, and the best one of all wasn't even real. Mike Myers, as Wayne Campbell, and Dana Carvey, as Garth Algar, sat in Wayne's Aurora, Illinois, basement and spouted off to a *Saturday Night Live* audience about everything from babes to new slang. *Schwing! Not! Babe alert! I think I'm gonna hurl! Do not blow chunks, Garth.* If you were over ten and under forty in the 1990s, you said at least one of those, probably more times than you'd like to admit.

The best *Wayne's World* bits illuminated the weird little private corners of Wayne and Garth's lives. Bruce Willis played the coolest senior in school introducing that year's cool word. ("Sphincter.") Wayne's mom (Nora Dunn) stopped by to lecture her son on how he always managed to spill everything on his T-shirts.

As the skit grew more popular, Wayne and Garth's world got bigger. Aerosmith visited their tiny little public-access show, and in the 1992 movie, Wayne fell for the babe-alicious Tia Carrere. But no amount of fame or star power could top two pals on a ratty couch, cracking wise and cracking each other up.

STATUS: Dana Carvey has said he'd do another movie, and that it's all up to Mike Myers. In the meantime, movie stoner pals Harold and Kumar have the same kind of sarcastic, smart-mouthed friendship Wayne and Garth once had.

FUN FACT: Myers and Carvey reprised their roles on *Saturday Night Live* in 2011. They couldn't stop laughing at the film title *Winter's Bone*. Schwing!

Whassup? Ads

Like beer consumption itself, Budweiser's Whassup? ads started out harmless and fun, but with repetition, turned head-poundingly painful.

The ads, which debuted in 1999, feature buddies yakking on the phone and screeching "Whassup?" at each other in drawn-out, cartoonish voices. Part of their charm was the unrehearsed sense of pure guyness—the friends were so amused by their own silliness, so consumed by their own World of Bro. The beer was there, but it was almost an afterthought. They might as well have been selling telephones.

When the ad took off, so did the catchphrase, making it impossible to go anywhere without a shrieked "Whassup?" causing your ears to bleed. The ad begat sequels—in one, a meal at a Japanese restaurant turns "Whassup?" into "Wasabi?" with a sushi chef chorus joining in.

But the best sequel showed a group of yuppies who, instead of "watchin' the game, havin' a Bud," were "watching the market recap, drinking an import." Instead of "Whassup?" their greeting was a stiff and proper "What are you doing?" The final scene cut to the original "Whassup?" guys staring at the screen in shocked disbelief.

STATUS: Budweiser is always cranking out new ads, some featuring the beloved Clydesdales. In 2010, they started using the slogan, "Grab Some Buds."

FUN FACT: In 2008, the guys were brought back for a pro-Obama ad. One is stationed in Iraq, another is unemployed, one's wearing multiple casts, and another is watching his stocks drop. In the end, the first guy watches Barack and Michelle Obama on TV, smiles, and says, "Change. That's what's up."

"Whatever"

Mom tells you you'll get gum disease if you don't floss? Whatever. Your sister whines that you got your ears double pierced at twelve so she should be able to get them single pierced at ten? What. Ev. Er. Your cousin argues that Jonathan Taylor Thomas is way cuter than Leonardo DiCaprio? Whatevs. W/E. Evs!

"Whatever" started to gain momentum with the Valley Girls of the 1980s, but really found its sneering, dismissive stride with children of the '90s. It is to conversation what Dan Dierdorf was to football—a good solid blocker. When you don't want to let a discussion go one step further, when all hope for progress is lost, or when you just really want to punch a blabby somebody in the mouth but it's not socially acceptable to do so, pull out the "whatever."

Kids, from toddlers to teenagers, have very little control over their lives. Bigger people make them do things, go places, say things they would never choose on their own. But "whatever" is the final bomb dropped on a verbal battle you can't or don't want to win.

No one can offer up a decent response. Other than "Don't 'whatever' me, young lady!" (Mom), there's just not a single verbal comeback that makes sense. Like Rhett Butler sailing out of Scarlett's life for the final time, you've expressed the amount of damns you give about this matter, and that amount is zero.

STATUS: You seriously think our language will ever give this one up? Whatever.

FUN FACT: "Whatever" was voted the most annoying word in the English language for three consecutive years in a Marist College poll.

Where's Waldo?

Kids like to find stuff. Parents like to keep kids quiet. Thus *Where's Waldo?* books hit the parent-kid sweet spot in a big way. No reading skills were required, only working eyeballs and a tiny bit of patience.

Being kids, we were good with the eyesight, but sometimes lacking in the "patience" realm. *Waldo* artist Martin Handford crammed hundreds of characters into his frustratingly detailed drawings, confusing the issue by throwing in red-and-white striped beach balls and other objects that closely resemble dorky Waldo's striped sweater and hat.

Why is Waldo wearing a sweater and long pants on the beach anyway? How come he constantly needs to be found? He appears to be under forty, so why does he walk with a cane? Also, does he have reverse claustrophobia? He never shows up in a crowd smaller

than forty gajillion, as if he perennially lives in the toy section of Walmart on Black Friday. More than just being found, he needed to be forcibly steered into some therapy.

STATUS: Waldo is everywhere, but he's still tough to spot.

FUN FACT: In the UK where he began, Waldo is called Wally. He's Walter in German, Charlie in French, Willy in Norwegian, and Volli in Estonian.

Windows 95

Our parents had to walk miles barefoot through the snow, uphill both ways, to get to their one-room schoolhouse—or so they say. But '90s kids had it almost as bad, trying to figure out the revolutionary but confusing Windows 95 operating system. Concepts that seem no-duh to us today (files you drag to the recycle bin stick around unless you empty it) had to be explained in painstaking detail. Looking back, we want to slap ourselves silly with a floppy disk.

Wait, what? We could name our files whatever we wanted?

Minimize a document and go back to it without having to reopen? Copy and paste? Hold us back from this futuristic technology! It was like being taken out of arithmetic and tossed into advanced algebra.

Thankfully, we had some, er, Friends to walk us through it. Microsoft hired sitcom stars Matthew Perry and Jennifer Aniston to star in an infamous video (available on VHS, natch) to teach us about this newfangled way of computing—and cheesily crack wise in the process. "Task bar?" asks Aniston. "Is that anything like a Snickers bar? Does it have nougat?" Ohhhh, man. No wonder Ross kept dumping her.

The media blitz for Windows 95 was unprecedented and will likely be unequaled. A new version, Windows 98, was in stores before some of us had even mastered emptying the recycling bin. Since then, programmers have been firing updates at us like fastballs in a batting cage, and sometimes it feels as if we're ducking more than we're keeping up. But there's no choice now. At work, home, and school, we're up at bat every day.

STATUS: Microsoft eventually ditched the year-naming convention, but years later, many features that were introduced in Windows 95 live on.

FUN FACT: The refrain of the Rolling Stones' "Start Me Up," the song Microsoft used in its ad campaign, is "You make a grown man cry"—a fact not lost on Windows 95 critics.

WWJD Bracelets

WWJD bracelets, with the initials standing for "What Would Jesus Do?" caught fire via Christian youth groups in the early 1990s, but were soon everywhere. Quickly, there were bumper stickers, T-shirts, lanyards, teddy bears, and, because this was still the '90s, even slap bracelets bearing the slogan.

You didn't have to be Christian to wear them, as the bracelets became a middle-school fashion craze, regardless of one's faith. Some kids doubled up on the wrist religion, wearing two or three at a time for extra questioning power.

Soon, the parodies took over. What Would Journey Do? What Would Brian Boitano Do? What Would Jesus Drive? What Would Scooby Do?

What *Would* Jesus Do? Whatever it was, he probably wouldn't bother to make a jewelry line about it.

STATUS: Not as popular, but still available.

FUN FACT: There's a follow-up bracelet with initials that purport to answer the WWJD question—FROG, for Fully Rely on God.

The X-Files

The sci-fi-and-supernatural mythology that ran through *The X-Files* was so thick, it turned off some viewers, but millions of nerds still tuned in every Friday night for their weekly dose of government conspiracies, alien-invasion plots, and scenes of people running with flashlights through shadowy Vancouver forests.

Most of us followed the show for the Sam-and-Diane-meet-E.T. chemistry between skeptical scientist Dana Scully and believer and porn aficionado Fox Mulder. But we also craved the creepy phenomena of the week, like the guy who could slither through narrow air vents, the serial killer who was really a demon, or Jesse "The Body" Ventura as a bulky Man in Black. And the topper, an episode that was so unsettling and horrific, it was banned from being rerun: "Home," where the inbred mutant family kept their legless and armless mother on a cart under the bed. Yeesh.

But if the (sometimes unsettling) fan fiction on the Internet is any indication, the answer most X-Philes longed for was when the heck Scully and Mulder were going to finally get it on. The duo did eventually lock lips—starting with a New Year's Eve smooch in 1999. Was it the right move to resolve all that sexual tension? The question has sparked more debate than the Roswell UFO crash, the moon landing hoax, and Elvis still being alive put together.

STATUS: *X* first marked the spot on the big screen in 1998, with the confusing *The X-Files: Fight the Future.* We wanted to believe, but even we couldn't comprehend how we spent five bucks on a movie that was mostly about bees and corn. A sequel followed ten years later.

FUN FACT: Mulder's sister Samantha was abducted while watching the 1970s show *The Magician*, the same show Patty Hearst was watching when she was kidnapped in 1974.

X Games

Anything the Olympics could do, the X Games could do backward on a skateboard launched from a helicopter while chugging a Red Bull. And with a pierced tongue. When the extreme sports competition began in 1995, a whole generation of snotty-nosed Evel Knievels skated into the spotlight as if it were an empty pool. Move aside, Bruce Jenner and Nadia Comaneci. Unlikely athletes like skateboarder Tony Hawk, and later, snowboarder Shaun White, took all the insane tricks kids were attempting on American playgrounds and mountains, perfected them, and then performed them on camera.

Even those of us who couldn't manage to skateboard the length of our block were fascinated by the televised spectacle. It was like a freak show you didn't have to feel bad about watching—seriously, did that guy just do a double back-flip on a snowmobile? X Games stars did everything your mom warned you against, and instead of getting grounded and ending up in traction, they got medals and ended up on Wheaties boxes. Throughout the whole thing, there rang a sense of generational pride. These weren't the Baby Boomer Games, after all. X marks the spot where sports married danger and gave birth to barely controlled insanity.

STATUS: Still extreeeeme!

FUN FACT: In 2004's *Harold & Kumar Go to White Castle*, a group of extreme sports freaks torment the film's stars, constantly shouting *"Extreme!"* At one point, they kayak through a convenience store.

Xena: Warrior Princess

Aye-yi-yi-yi-yi! Hercules may have been strong enough to knock out a giant with a single punch, but a busty gal in a skirt trounced his leather-pantsed butt in both TV ratings and cult popularity. *Xena: Warrior Princess*, the 1995–2001 spin-off of *Hercules: The Legendary Journeys*, followed the title character as she traveled around ancient Greece in a tiny outfit and some totally bitchin' bangs, trying to atone for her past as a jerk.

In 2007, *TV Guide* named *Xena* number ten on its list of the Top Cult Shows Ever, and rightfully so: Fans, especially those who knew their way around D&D dice and Renaissance festivals, flocked to the program because it mixed humor with good, old-fashioned sword and sorcery, blending historical fantasy with contemporary pop culture. (Aphrodite, goddess of love, talked like a Valley Girl—like, omigawd, that is a totally tubular toga.)

Xena was one of the first action shows to put an empowered woman front and center, paving the way for everybody from Buffy the Vampire Slayer to Sydney Bristow from *Alias* to Starbuck from *Battlestar Galactica*. Xena demanded respect; if you didn't play nice, she would slice your head off with a chakram, her signature round-bladed weapon. Even her traveling companion—Robin to her Batman—Gabrielle, evolved from a milquetoast to badass over the run of the show. The pair's relationship may have evolved into something else altogether, as well: It was never definitively confirmed, but there's been much speculation that Xena and Gabrielle were one of TV's first Ambiguously Gay Duos. You go, girls.

STATUS: The syndication gods killed the show (and Xena herself) in 2001, but she continues to live on in comic books, fan fiction, and on the convention circuit.

FUN FACT: Lucy Lawless donated her skimpy costume to the Smithsonian's Museum of American History.

Y2K Panic

Well, the planet had a good 4.5-billion-year run, but it was finally lights-out for Mother Earth. Thanks to the Y2K computer bug, life as we knew it was going to end exactly the way the Mayans predicted: at the hands of nerds.

Specifically, lazy code-writing nerds who let us get away with entering just two numerals to indicate a year, neglecting to account for what might happen when the millennium flipped over. Doomsayers predicted that when the clock ticked its last 1999 tock, computers would no longer understand what year it was, so they'd shut down. Planes would fall out of the sky. Nuclear missiles would launch. VCRs would flash 12:00. Party over—whoops, out of time.

Some people stocked up on food and water, hoarded cash, and barricaded themselves in bomb shelters and basements, watching Dick Clark count down to Armageddon. Others partied like it was 1999, and rang in the New Year as if it was their last hour on Earth, figuring they'd be able to better weather the collapse of society if they were really drunk.

So what happened? Nothing. The ball dropped, the computers figured it out, and the embarrassed people who overreacted spent the next year eating the three hundred cans of Dinty Moore Beef Stew they'd stashed in the cellar.

STATUS: No longer a worry. Until the year 20,000, at which time our alien overlords can figure it out.

Zima

Poor Zima. Its maker, Coors, tried to ride the clear beverage wave of the early 1990s, but the one thing that wasn't clear was why you would buy the stuff. It wasn't beer. It wasn't wine. It wasn't a wine cooler. The massive $50-million advertising campaign didn't seem to know what it was either, desperately declaring, "It's Zomething different."

Sure, if "Zomething" means it tastes like flat Sprite, or metallic gin and tonic. Coors wanted an audience of men, but the drink with the cute name and fashion-forward bottle caught on more with women instead. And not that many of them. Comic David Letterman helped seal Zima's doom with constant jabs, pitching it as the preferred drink of nutty senators, confused marathoners, and oddly, Santa.

Coors tried to rejigger the drink with fruity flavors but

Zomethings just can't be Zaved. Zima's short life and thoroughly bizarre concept earned it a permanent place in the hall of fame of only-in-the-'90s products. Call it the Big Mouth Billy Bass of booze.

STATUS: Long gone. Mike's Hard Lemonade now has a number of fruity malt beverages that are somewhat similar.

FUN FACT: According to Slate, college kids mixed Zima with schnapps and called the resulting drink "Nox-Zima."

Zines

In the days before blogs, webpages, and Twitter feeds let everyone have their say, creative writers and editors who longed to be heard turned to the low-tech tools of good old-fashioned paper and scissors and created zines, small-circulation independent magazines.

For a reader, finding the zine that spoke to your own personal obsession wasn't as easy as pecking out a Google search. You might use *Factsheet 5* or other zine review publications to narrow down your choices, then pop a well-concealed buck or two into an SASE and wait for an individual zinester to mail you off a copy. Or you'd hit the smarter crop of comic-book and magazine stores, those that sold more than just *Batman* and *Better Homes and Gardens*, and raid the tiny stash of zines they propped on the bottom racks.

But once you had zine in hand and could kick back to enjoy, the hunt was worth it. Siblings Erin and Don Smith reveled in *Brady Bunch* nostalgia in the *Sassy* magazine–approved zine *Teenage Gang Debs*. *Giant Robot* celebrated Asian-American culture, from reviews of hot sauces to ruminations on Godzilla. *Infiltration* celebrated the underground world of sneaking into places where you're not supposed to go, such as storm drains and hotel pools. *Snackbar Confidential* mixed delightfully lurid drive-in theater ads from the 1970s with weirdly creepy photos of cereal mascots.

These were topics—and typos—that perhaps would never have made it past an assignment editor at a major newspaper or slick magazine. But reading them was pure joy, the print equivalent of stumbling upon a musical genius who never hit it big, but who made uncannily on-target music for those brave enough to seek it out.

STATUS: Some zines turned into full-fledged magazines, but the topics and fierce personalities of many are now reflected online.

Zubaz

Between grungy flannels and Zubaz, you'd think everyone in the 1990s dressed like it was perennially Laundry Day.

Zubaz were created in 1998 by two Minnesota weightlifters who needed workout pants to fit their massive thighs. So they were pretty much tapered-leg sweatpants, but sweatpants that were born inside a whirring spin-paint machine. You could also buy the zebra-patterned pants in your school colors or those of your favorite sports team, which resulted in wearers walking around looking like they were dressed as packs of Fruit Stripe gum.

If you wore Zubaz and it wasn't because you needed them for that daily bench-press contest at the gym, you probably had given up on fashion about the time Nehru jackets went out of style. Sure, they were comfy, but to every female on the planet, they screamed, "Here is a man who does not care what he wears. And also might be legally blind."

STATUS: The weightlifters who started Zubaz brought the clothing line back in 2008.

FUN FACT: In 1993, *Inside Sports* magazine picked Zubaz as third on their annual list of "Worst Things to Happen to Sports."

Acknowledgments

Thanks to all the people who contributed ideas, fun stuff to photograph, and other support, including:

Jen, Rory, and Maddy Bellmont
Rob and Kelly Cooper
Bob and Karen Bellmont
Ann and Ed Fashingbauer
Chris and Katie Bellmont
Dave Bellmont and Tara Weatherly
Don and Nancy Bellmont
Jeff and Mari Bellmont
Kevin and Molly Bellmont
Mike and Ryan Bellmont
Nick Bellmont and Angela Determan
Reed and Ryan Bisson
Claudia Fashingbauer
Eric and Allison Guggisberg
Kelsey Guggisberg and Ricky Schroeder
Anne and Tom Howard
Clio and Carl McLagan

Molly McLagan

Annie-marie and Mark Miller

Grace Peters

Bridget Sitzer and Dan Nordlund

Gretchen Sitzer

Patrick Sitzer

Isaac Welle

Shelli Lissick, Bridget Nelson Monroe, Tara Cegla, Megan
Swenson, David Hlavac, and Sheri O'Meara at Bellmont
Partners

Steve Volavka, Kristina Murto, and Brent Thomas at Ensemble
Creative & Marketing

Staff at Jewel Box Café, Seattle

Everybody who hangs out at GenXtinct.com and facebook.com/
genxtinct

Index

Page numbers in *italic* indicate photographs.

About the Authors

Gael Fashingbauer Cooper is a journalist who writes the nationally recognized pop culture blog *Pop Culture Junk Mail*.

Brian Bellmont is a former television reporter and producer who now runs a public relations agency.

Visit their website at www.genxtinct.com or www.facebook.com/genxtinct.